KNITTING WITH
NOVELTY YARNS

KNITTING WITH
NOVELTY YARNS

Exploring Color, Texture, and Style

LAURA MILITZER BRYANT AND BARRY KLEIN

Martingale™
& COMPANY

CREDITS

President · Nancy J. Martin
CEO/Publisher · Daniel J. Martin
Associate Publisher · Jane Hamada
Editorial Director · Mary V. Green
Editorial Project Manager · Tina Cook
Technical Editor · Ursula Reikes
Copy Editor · Liz McGehee
Design and Production Manager · Stan Green
Illustrator · Robin Strobel
Cover and Text Designer · Trina Stahl
Fashion Photography · Anna Midori Abe
Hair and Makeup · Shannon Rasheed
Fashion Stylist · Emilie Maslow
Detail Photography · Brent Kane

Knitting with Novelty Yarns: Exploring Color,
Texture, and Style
© 2001 by Laura Militzer Bryant and Barry Klein

Martingale & Company
20205 144th Ave. NE
Woodinville, WA 98072-8478 USA
www.martingale-pub.com

Printed in Hong Kong
06 05 04 03 02   8 7 6 5 4 3 2

MISSION STATEMENT

We are dedicated to providing quality products and service by working together to inspire creativity and to enrich the lives we touch.

Library of Congress Cataloging-in-Publication Data

Bryant, Laura.
    Knitting with novelty yarns / Laura Bryant and Barry Klein.
        p. cm.
    ISBN 1-56477-357-4
        1. Knitting—Patterns. 2. Novelty fabrics. 3. Yarn.
        I. Klein, Barry.- II. Title.

TT825 .B79 2001
778.9'328—dc21   2001016247

DEDICATION

To the spirit of adventuresome knitters everywhere

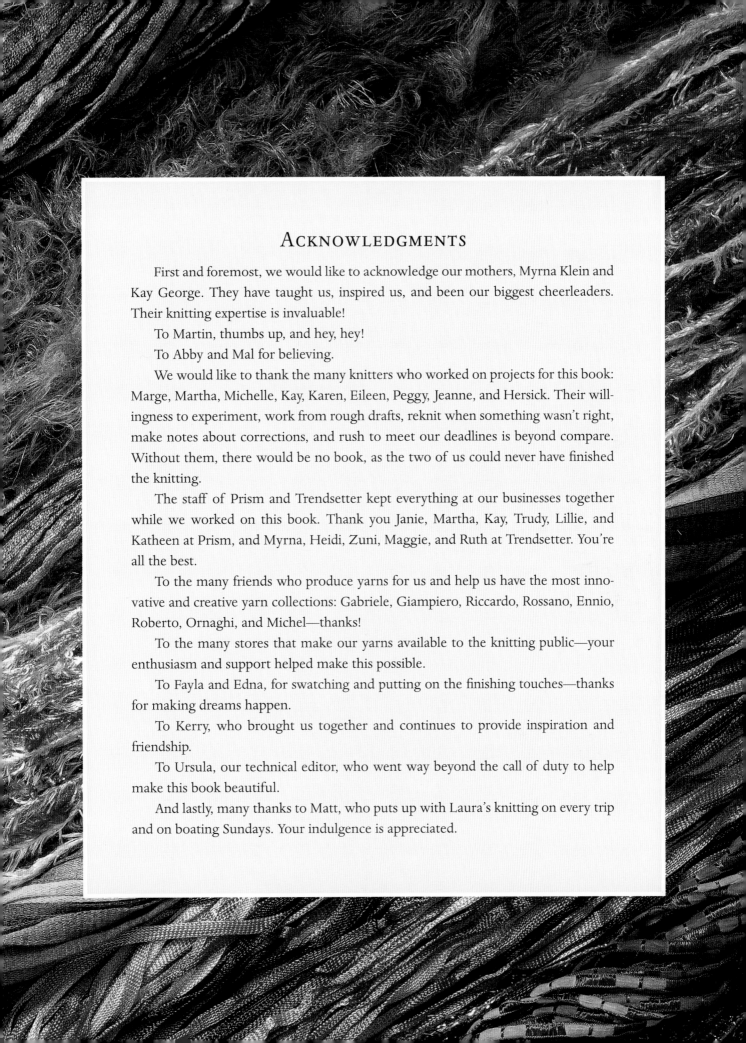

ACKNOWLEDGMENTS

First and foremost, we would like to acknowledge our mothers, Myrna Klein and Kay George. They have taught us, inspired us, and been our biggest cheerleaders. Their knitting expertise is invaluable!

To Martin, thumbs up, and hey, hey!

To Abby and Mal for believing.

We would like to thank the many knitters who worked on projects for this book: Marge, Martha, Michelle, Kay, Karen, Eileen, Peggy, Jeanne, and Hersick. Their willingness to experiment, work from rough drafts, reknit when something wasn't right, make notes about corrections, and rush to meet our deadlines is beyond compare. Without them, there would be no book, as the two of us could never have finished the knitting.

The staff of Prism and Trendsetter kept everything at our businesses together while we worked on this book. Thank you Janie, Martha, Kay, Trudy, Lillie, and Katheen at Prism, and Myrna, Heidi, Zuni, Maggie, and Ruth at Trendsetter. You're all the best.

To the many friends who produce yarns for us and help us have the most innovative and creative yarn collections: Gabriele, Giampiero, Riccardo, Rossano, Ennio, Roberto, Ornaghi, and Michel—thanks!

To the many stores that make our yarns available to the knitting public—your enthusiasm and support helped make this possible.

To Fayla and Edna, for swatching and putting on the finishing touches—thanks for making dreams happen.

To Kerry, who brought us together and continues to provide inspiration and friendship.

To Ursula, our technical editor, who went way beyond the call of duty to help make this book beautiful.

And lastly, many thanks to Matt, who puts up with Laura's knitting on every trip and on boating Sundays. Your indulgence is appreciated.

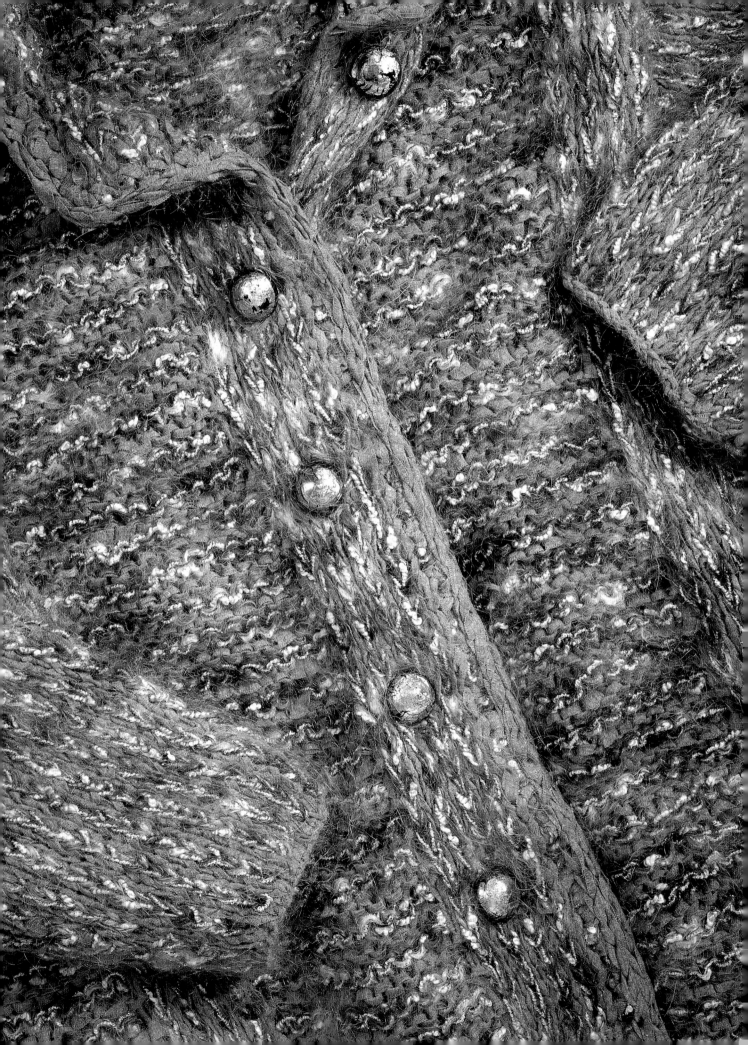

CONTENTS

A TALE OF
TWO KNITTERS

EVERYONE FOLLOWS a different path in his or her life, and we are no exception. We came to write this book through richly varied backgrounds that took us through immeasurable experiences. Some of our backgrounds overlap; others diverge. As we each found our path and eventually found each other, a wonderful synergy took place. Although our companies remain separate, we work closely, especially in research and development. We hope you enjoy our journey—and that we inspire you on your own.

Barry Klein and Laura Militzer Bryant

LAURA MILITZER BRYANT

I began knitting at a young age—my mother taught me when I was eight years old. I took to it right away, often making presents for my friends and family. The entrepreneurial spirit hit me early, and in my teens I produced crocheted miniskirts and purses for a local boutique. College led me from prelaw to art school, where I flourished, picking up business skills from a bookkeeping job for the Dean's Assistant, and critical thinking from a variety of excellent teachers.

A concentration in textiles produced a budding artist who wanted nothing more than to make and sell artwork. My weavings, which I still pursue, are large scale, time-consuming, and not production oriented (each piece is original), and it quickly became apparent that making a living selling artwork was not very realistic. I had several bookkeeping jobs and eventually wound up in a retail yarn store as a clerk and finisher. While there, I became aware of the variety of products in the market. A visiting sales representative told me of an area that was becoming available for a number of good yarn lines, so I talked my way into a sales-rep position. As an independent representative, I called on stores all over New York State and attended the National Needlework Association (TNNA) trade shows.

A whole new world of yarn opened up to me. For the first time, I saw hand-dyed knitting yarns, and I realized that I could do that too! My strong background in the technical aspects of dyeing (all of my weavings are hand dyed and painted) and an equally strong background in color theory (I have studied and taught color for twenty-two years) made the prospect seem simple. I approached Diane Friedman of Tahki Yarns, one of the lines I represented, and proposed hand dyeing colors for their wool tweed line by overdyeing the pale tweeds for a look that would be different from any currently available. She agreed, and we began a long and fruitful endeavor. Prism was born and began its own evolution.

Eventually, I became interested in dyeing different yarns, acquiring mohair and cottons from England, angora from France, and silk from Switzerland, while Tahki discontinued their hand-dyed yarns. Because Prism was small and could respond quickly, we became known for unusual and cutting-edge fibers. We were the first to show eyelash, six months prior to anyone else—we received the sample yarn one week before a show, knitted a quick sweater, and took orders! But also because we were small, many people didn't know about us. A persistent sales representative from the West Coast, Kerry Adams, convinced me after several years of courtship that we were ready to grow and that she could help. She became my first sales rep, and she

was right! Prism has continued to expand and now employs four sales reps who cover fairly large territories. We also exhibit at two major trade shows, publish up to four pattern books per year, and service about two hundred and fifty stores across North America. Six full-time employees wind, tie, and label the yarns that are, to this day, dyed by me alone.

Kerry was instrumental in Prism's direction in another way, too. In the late 1980s, one of my sources went out of business, leaving me unable to obtain certain products. Kerry introduced me to Barry Klein of Trendsetter Yarns. Barry was able to help me replace the products in question, and as our friendship and working relationship developed, he became invaluable to me in obtaining new yarns. We share technical knowledge, brainstorming, and inspiration on an almost daily basis. I talked Barry into joining me as a teacher at the Knitting Guild of America conventions; Barry cajoled me into becoming active in TNNA. We often design using each other's yarns, and believe that what is good for one is good for the other and for the industry and craft of knitting as a whole. Our shared interest in novelty yarns has been the basis for this book. Years of designing with unusual yarns has given us a wealth of knowledge—information we were eager to share with others. We hope our experiences make yours more fruitful and satisfying.

Writing this book with Barry has been a trial and a joy. The creative energy flowing was phenomenal; the long hours and frustrations to get it all just right were taxing—but worth the effort. I think this collaboration is headed for a long life and will produce more projects of joy and celebration. We hope you enjoy our adventures as well.

BARRY KLEIN

It is safe to say that knitting is in my blood and that working with my hands has been a lifelong happening. I came into this business at the age of seven, when my mother opened a retail needlework store. I spent my afternoons in the store looking at the fibers and playing with different yarns—it was that or do my homework. I learned how to needlepoint from Elsa Williams, the founding mother of the needlework industry.

As knitting became fashionable, one of the stores employee's, Sylvia, taught me to knit. I was in love and knew that being able to create something with my hands was incredible. Everyone in the store learned the art of custom charting, and we created specialty sweaters and designs for our customers. At the same time, my mother expanded her interests and started Fantacia, one of the first true novelty yarn companies in the United States. I went to a local college and took classes in marketing and television arts, and at the same time, began designing Fantacia's collection of sweater patterns. When the opportunity presented itself to become a sales agent for the company, I jumped at the chance to travel, meet customers, and sell the yarns I worked with.

After finishing college, I knew I had a career ahead of me. I was hooked on creating fashion, working with store owners, and helping the knitters who purchased the yarns. Fantacia closed, and so my mother, Myrna, and I decided to start something new and fresh. As a result, Trendsetter Yarns was born. Working with many of the same factories as Fantacia and searching out new ones, we put a mission on paper: bring the most exciting and innovative collection of novelty yarns to knitters in the United States. I am fortunate to work with some of the most wildly creative yarn companies in Italy and France. They allow me to see yarns in the works and add the touches that make Trendsetter Yarns so special. I get to create yarns from scratch, select colors, name them, design packaging, and set the skein size. Most yarns take about two years from conception to distribution, and they are all my children.

In order to sell my yarns, I belong to the National Needlework Association, a trade organiza-tion that puts on trade markets for retail store own-ers. In addition to selling at markets, we have won-derful educational programs and special events that I have participated in. I have been on the board of directors for the past six years, and president for the last four years, bringing my love of needlework to our association and helping us move toward wider acceptance and a broader view of marketing our industry.

Over the years, I have been privileged to make friends around the United States who share my pas-sion for knitting. My customers have allowed me to visit their stores and work with them by teaching classes, setting up trunk shows, and inspiring their customers. I have also been a featured teacher for the Knitting Guild and Stitches conferences. These friendships are a blessing and something that I truly cherish.

What cannot be passed over is the best blessing of all: meeting Laura almost eleven years ago at a needlework show. I had seen many of the beautiful yarns that Laura was dyeing but had never met her. Kerry Adams, one of our shared sales agents, brought us together one day, just knowing that we had to meet. From the first conversation until today, we have not stopped talking about yarns, designs, and textures. Laura has inspired me to broaden my thoughts on design and to be more open to experi-mentation with color. Laura has also made this book one of the most joyous and exciting projects I have ever worked on.

The future holds some really exciting new proj-ects as well. As knitting becomes more popular, our yarn collection heads in new directions. We work on our collection about two years in advance, so I can promise you more of the same along with some wonderful new surprises. Sit tight and keep your eyes open. Please join us as we keep knitting alive.

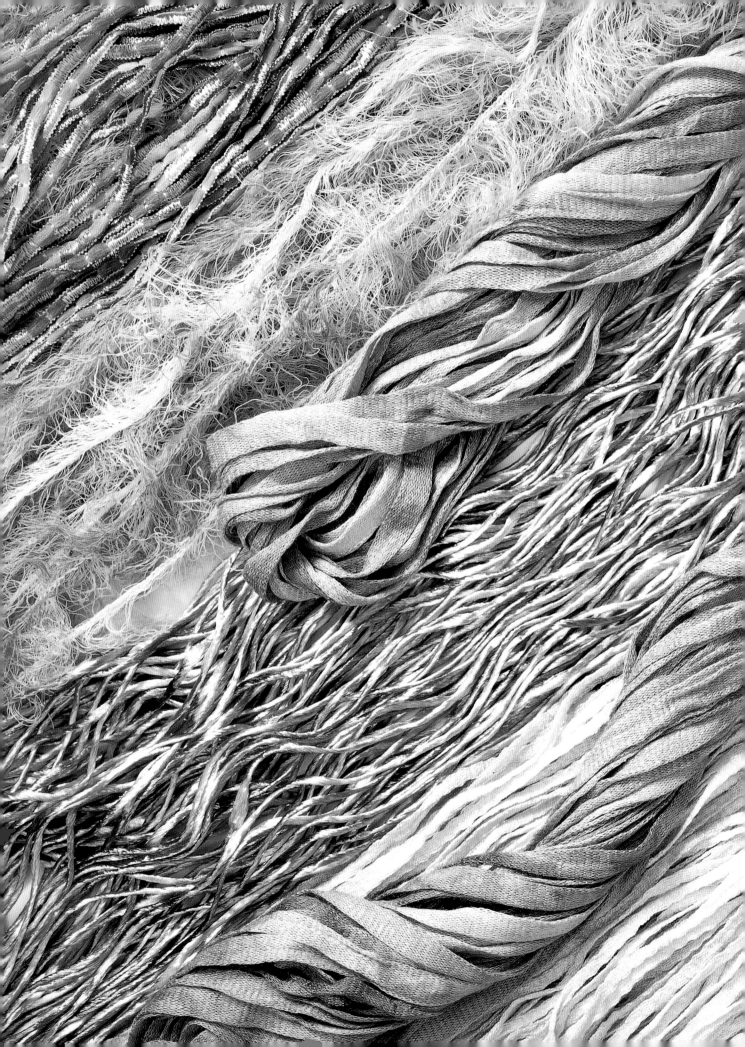

FIBERS, YARN TYPES, AND THEIR CHARACTERISTICS

THE WORD "textile" can be used to define a knit or woven fabric, or the yarns that are used in the creation of the fabric. Yarns are constructed from fibers: natural or man-made filaments or hairs, or blended fibers that have been combined into a thicker strand. Each fiber type can be found in various yarns, including bouclé, brushed, chained, chenille, component, eyelash, knitted, nub, plied, and woven. Before we begin the discussion about yarn construction, it is useful to know something about the variety of fibers that can be made into yarn.

Animal Fibers

These fibers come directly from animals. Since the animal used the fiber as its clothing, these fibers have superior qualities of insulation and breathability. The fur, when sheared or plucked, will then be spun into a yarn that retains the same characteristics that it had for the animal. Because animals come in a variety of colors, the natural color of the fiber is often retained. At the same time, brilliant colors are also possible by dyeing the fiber with acid-based dyes.

Animal fibers are comfortable and nonallergenic to most people. Often someone who thinks they are allergic to wool is actually sensitive to the chemicals used to process the fiber. It is common practice to dissolve plant fibers (burrs, etc.) from animal fibers by using sulfuric acid. (In the past this was done by carding and combing the fibers.) Residual acid remains in the fiber; because the fiber is warm, you may perspire, and even slight moisture activates the acid, which in turn "picks" your skin. Handspun yarns, whose fleece has also been hand carded, and hand-dyed yarns, whose dyeing process neutralizes the acid, can both be far more comfortable to wear. An itchy sweater can often be helped by handwashing and soaking in a mild solution of baking soda.

All animal fibers are subject to shrinking and felting when in the presence of friction and heat. Wool and angora are the most susceptible; alpaca and mohair most resistant. Because animal fibers can shrink and felt, they must be hand washed in cool water and handled very gently—any temperature differential, wringing, or agitation will cause the individual filaments to felt together in a mass.

There are a number of different animals that share their fleece with us. The following paragraphs describe a variety of animal fibers available.

ANGORA

The hair is plucked from the Angora rabbit in clumps so that the small bulb at the end of the hair remains attached. The bulb helps anchor the hair when spun. Because of the time involved in removing the hair, Angora becomes one of the costliest fibers known by weight. Angora is also one of the warmest fibers known. As a result, the base fiber is often blended with wool to decrease both cost and excessive warmth. Angora is extremely soft and lofty, and has a tendency to shed.

ALPACA

The alpaca is a relative of the llama, and it is found mostly in the high mountains of Peru. Alpaca is long-stapled (meaning it has relatively long fibers), silky, and not as elastic as wool, leading to more stretch over time. Many alpaca yarns are found in their original color.

CASHMERE

One of the more costly fibers available today, cashmere comes from the cashmere goat. These animals are native to Tibet and roam the high mountains. The small number of animals leads to limited production, raising the cost. The yarn dyes beautifully and softens as it is worn. It has warmth, sheen, and a luxurious feel.

MOHAIR

The Angora goat gives up its hair so we can enjoy the beauty of mohair. The hairs are long-stapled, silky, and dye easily. Mohair is sometimes used as a blend with wool in traditional plied yarns, but it is most often found brushed. Kid mohair comes from young goats and is softer than adult mohair. Sweaters knit from brushed mohair are lightweight and airy, yet retain insulating qualities for warmth.

WOOL

There are many different varieties of wool. The base fiber is sheared from the fleece of a sheep. The feel and detail of wool varies with different breeds of sheep. Wool is the most common animal fiber used in yarns because of the abundance of sheep raised around the world and because of its superior qualities for spinning and dyeing. The natural crimp in wool fibers leads to spun yarns that are elastic and retain their shape well.

Plant Fibers

This type of fiber comes directly from plants that are grown in the soil. Since the earth is used as the generator, weather, soil conditions, altitude, and water can affect the quality and quantity of plant fiber that is produced. Different regions around the world specialize in different types of plant fibers. Alkaline-based dyes are used to dye plant fibers. Some of the common forms of plant fibers are discussed in this section, including silk.

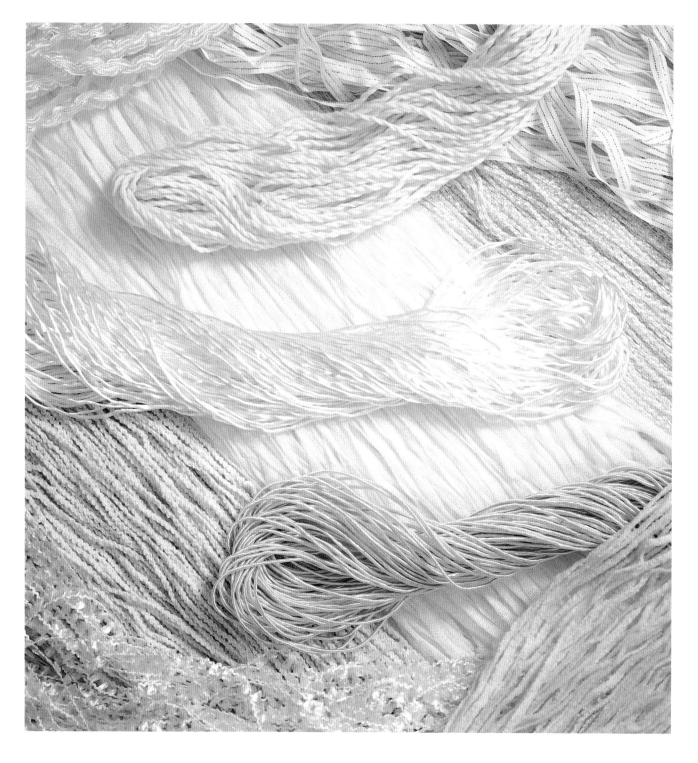

Cotton

Cotton tufts or bulbs come from the boll of the cotton plant. Warm weather and light rainfall are best for the production of cotton. The fiber spins easily, and yarns made in cotton are soft, absorbent, and breathable. When plied, cotton has great strength and lots of weight. Raw cotton has a rough, rustic character to it. Cotton may be mercerized, a process of treating the fiber with lye that causes it to shrink and become very shiny. Mercerized cotton is more stable than raw cotton, will pill less, and takes dye more readily, resulting in brilliant colors. Cotton tends to stretch but will return to its original shape with dry heat.

Rayon

Also known as viscose, rayon does not exist as a natural fiber. It is extruded from processed wood pulp and shares many characteristics with other natural fibers. It can have a matte finish, but most often has a sheen, and takes dye quickly and easily. Because rayon can be heavy, it is often found blended with wool or nylon. Rayon is very strong and is often used for nubs and slubs because of this, yet it weakens when wet. Rayon yarns tend to stretch permanently, so garments should be made a bit smaller with this in mind.

Linen

Linen comes directly from the flax plant and is a strong, long, fibrous filament. Linen has been a staple fiber throughout history because of its strength. Dull by nature, linen does not take dye easily and the colors are usually quite matte. Unlike rayon, linen is actually stronger when wet, which speaks to its long history as a working fiber. Woven linen fabrics are prone to wrinkles, but knitted fabric is less so. Usually crisp when first worked with, linen softens with handling.

Silk

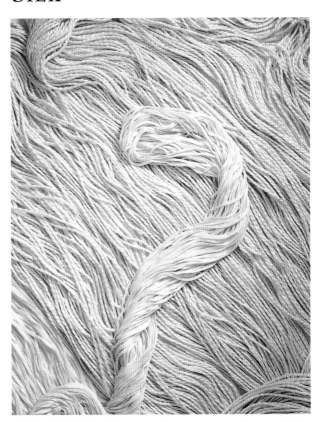

Silk is a hybrid of plant and animal fibers because it is composed of plant material processed by an animal. Silk fiber, spun from the deconstructed cocoons of the silk worm, can be dyed with either acid-based or alkaline-based dyes. It has been known as a luxury fiber throughout history. Fabrics woven from fine silk threads are some of the most valued textiles; however, yarns spun from silk are heavy, have a tendency to pill, and have no resilience. Silk yarns can be improved by blending with cotton or wool. Chained yarns made from fine silk threads will not pill, but they still have little resilience, and will stretch over time.

Synthetic Fibers

Synthetic fibers are man-made and usually petroleum-based. The process of creating synthetic fibers requires extrusion, resulting in yarns that are microscopically dense and don't breathe well. Synthetic fibers are widely used in many novelty yarns because production is unlimited and so is the variety of ways the fibers can be manipulated. The synthetic fibers described in this section are just a few of the varieties available.

ACRYLIC

This yarn will go down in history with a bad image because when first created, the yarn had a plastic sheen and a hard finish. We often joke about the yarn coming from the "Acryl," a local farm animal, in order to add mystique. Used mostly for afghans and children's garments, acrylic takes dye well and washes with ease. However, repeated laundering will eventually wear the yarn out and cause garments to pill and appear limp and lifeless. Acrylic is used as a blending fiber to lower cost, increase washability, and add lightness.

POLYESTER

Polyester is used mostly in nub yarns, eyelash yarns, woven ribbons, and other novelties because the base fiber is extremely fine and strong and can be plied to any thickness. Polyester provides an inexpensive way to add luster.

NYLON

Nylon is the stabilizing fiber in many knitting yarns. The strength of spun nylon makes this fiber one of the most widely used binder yarns because it holds plies together, keeps nubs in place, hooks bouclé loops, and still allows the yarn to remain soft. Nylon takes the same dyes as those used for wool, with the same brilliance. It is silky, drapable, and chameleon-like in its ability to take on many different looks—matte, shiny, smooth, papery, plastic—which makes it the fiber of choice for many different novelty constructions.

Yarn Types

When we decide on a yarn, we examine many different characteristics. Laura hand dyes her yarns so she must consider how specific dyes will take. For Barry, the fiber type is not as important because he works with many different factories who are able to dye different fibers. For both of us, the important aspects of each yarn we select are appearance, hand, and resilience. Hand involves the total feel of a yarn in the skein, while knitting, and in the final fabric— soft or crisp, limp or firm, thick or thin, spongy or stiff. The resilience factor determines how the yarn will hold up during knitting and when worn. We ask ourselves many questions when considering a new yarn. How is the look of the yarn affected by needle size? Are there stitches that will enhance durability and feel? Can the yarn be washed? What is the strength of the fiber, and how flexible will it be for the design we envision? Is it pleasant to knit with? Does it have an unusual look? Who will want to knit with it? While most of our yarns are sold for hand knitting, we are finding our yarns used in crochet, tassels, wallpaper, woven fabrics, hair ribbons, jewelry, embroidery, needlepoint, stationery, and more.

Successful knitting involves developing a sense for which yarn will work well for the design you have selected. Production runs of novelty yarns last about two years. Patterns are timeless. As a result, if you know what yarn type was used for the pattern you have chosen, you can substitute another yarn that will give similar results. You can also learn to make subtle changes in patterns by switching yarns that match in gauge, but will impart a different look. The chapter titled "The Flock Exchange" gives you a firsthand look at this process. We exchange yarns for each other's designs and then explain our selection and how the overall look of the finished design is affected.

In the meantime, let's talk about textiles and the styles of yarns that are common to the designs that we work with. For each type of yarn, look through your private stash and walk through the process. If you don't have a particular yarn, you may want to go to your local yarn store and get a skein. Having a sample to play with helps you understand the yarn and its construction.

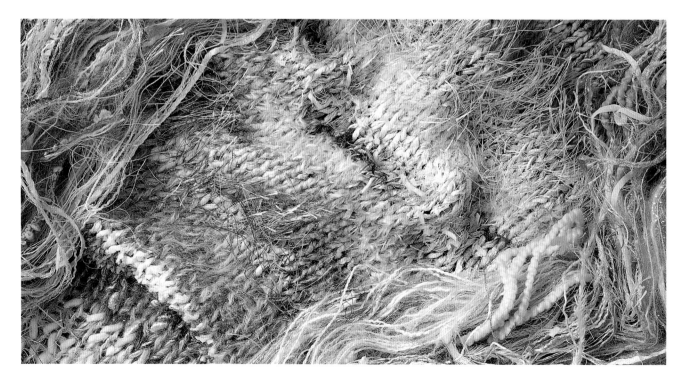

BOUCLÉ YARNS

A bouclé yarn has a very special look and is based on the creation of small, medium, or large loops during the spinning process. A base fiber is run through a spinning machine. At regular intervals, the machine stops pulling the fiber, but the flow of yarn through the head of the spindle continues, creating a loop. The length of time that the pulling is stopped determines loop size. To keep the loop in place, a support thread is wrapped around or chained into the yarn. Take a sample of bouclé and look at the end. You will see the yarn that creates the bouclé effect and a support fiber, which is usually thin nylon or polyester. As you unravel the yarn, imagine it being pulled through the machine.

Bouclé yarns can be created with many different types of fibers because the binder provides strength. The appearance is usually thick and bulky, making complicated stitch patterns unnecessary. Slip-stitch patterns are successful when using a ribbon or smooth yarn in contrast, allowing the full texture of the bouclé to show. As with many textured yarns, most of the detail from the loops is found on the purl side. Garter stitch, reverse stockinette, and slip-stitch patterns show off the texture best.

For the consummate knitter, working with bouclé yarns can be a pleasure, but less experienced knitters may have a tougher time. There is a tendency to pick up a loop of yarn, rather than the stitch, with the point of your needle, which can create a bit of frustration, or even worse, add extra stitches to your knitting. Using a needle size that is one or two larger than expected can help, making it more difficult to pick up loops since the point of the needle is larger than the loop. With the support fiber keeping the loops in place, wool and mohair bouclé yarns tend to hold their shape no matter what needle size you use. For cotton and rayon bouclé, we recommend smaller needles because, by nature, these fibers are limp. With a smaller needle, the stitches will be denser and the knit fabric more firm.

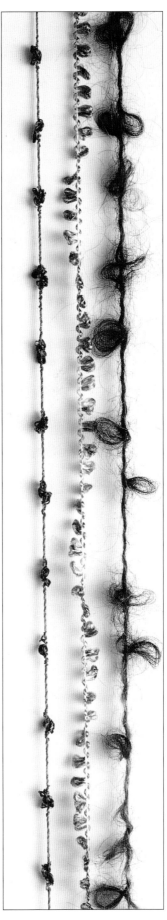

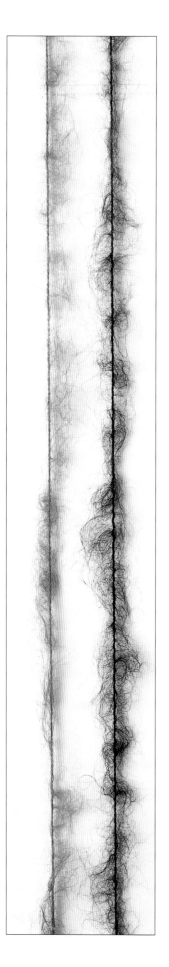

BRUSHED YARNS

YOU WOULD THINK that the name "brushed" says it all: you take out a brush and comb it. Yet to create a brushed yarn, it must start as a chained or bouclé yarn. What creates a brushed effect is the fact that it indeed goes through a brushing process. Like the teeth of a dog's brush, metal teeth are set on a round cylinder, and the yarns are then run over the teeth to brush up the base yarn.

A chained yarn is made in tubular fashion with a fiber that can be brushed. The strength of the chained yarn will hold up against the metal teeth pulling at it and will allow the brushed fiber to come up, creating a hair effect. A bouclé yarn is a looped yarn with a tight binder holding the loops in place. When this yarn is run against the teeth, it pulls the loop, creating a brushed effect of different lengths by breaking the loops.

Manufacturers use polyester, mohair, wool, nylon, angora, or acrylic, depending on the effect they desire, to create brushed yarns. Each yarn brushes differently, with acrylic and polyester giving a shiny look and the others imparting a more matte look. Brushed yarns achieve a fuzzy, light, and airy effect. If the yarn is space dyed, brushing the yarn will intermingle the layers of color, giving the knitting a new dimension. There are many options for stitch patterns. Textured stitches add more detail and may make the hair stand up even more. Intarsia or colored knitting is another good use of brushed yarns, especially when they are worked with twisted, flat, or ribbon yarns that enhance the texture by contrast. The strength added by the core, and the depth of a brushed hair allow most brushed yarns to be knit on larger needles than expected. The hairs fill in the open spaces and keep the knitting lighter.

CHAINED AND KNITTED YARNS

A circular bobbin with hooks coming out of the top, an I-cord machine, a French knitting spool—these are all variations, old and new, that create a chain or tube. The machines used to create chained yarn are high-powered machines with up to twelve hooks, or needles, in a circle. The number of needles used determines the thickness of the finished yarn. Chained yarns are typically thinner; as they become larger and more tubular, we refer to them as knitted tapes.

To make a chained tube, the yarn is fed from above, run through each hook, and chained in a circular flow. A weight or bobbin is added to the end, pulling the yarn through the base of the machine while keeping the chained stitches even. There is no restriction on the type of fibers used to create chained yarn: cotton, rayon, acetate, mohair, wool, microfiber, linen, metallic, and more.

If you take a sample of a chained yarn and blow on the end, it will open to expose the circle and you will be able to count the number of needles used. A chained yarn will run like pantyhose if the end is pulled or a stitch is broken. Be sure to secure the end carefully by knotting it or applying a small dab of clear nail polish or a special glue called FrayCheck. Knitting with chained yarn produces fabric that is usually very secure and tight. Many different types of textured stitches, cables, and slip-stitch patterns look good in chained yarns. Chained yarns can be heavy and thick with not much yardage. Because of the weight, they are often used as only part of a design, as ribbing, or as a camisole. Many new yarns contain microfibers, which allow for lighter weight and better yardage. Look at the fiber, weight, and yardage in any chained yarn you are contemplating buying to help determine if the yarn will work as planned.

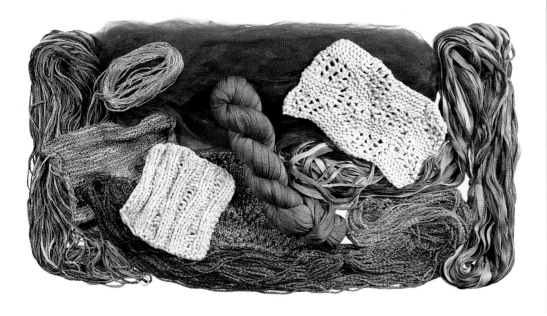

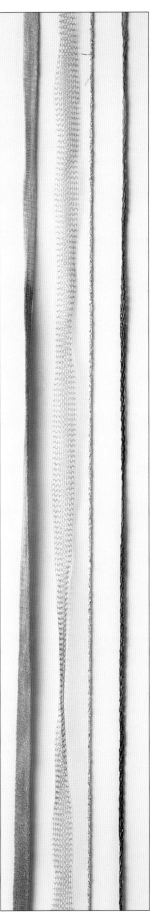

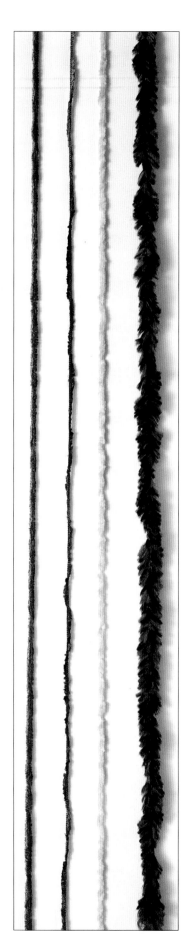

CHENILLE YARNS

THIS IS THE yarn that we all have a love/hate relationship with. The look and feel of chenille is luxurious. The attention to detail required while knitting and the short life of wearing the knit fabric make some people shy away from working with it.

Chenille is created on a circular spinning machine that has two heads. The narrow center head has a core fiber that is strong and twists at high speed. The outer head runs fiber in a circular motion through the center core, and the twisting locks it in place. The effect at this point is of loops that are locked at the center. These loops are pulled quickly against extremely sharp razors, cutting the loops and opening up the many plies of fiber. People complain that chenille sheds, yet the more it sheds, the better the quality of fiber used. To increase softness, more and finer plies are used to create the body yarn, so more ends are cut and opened up, allowing more shedding.

Because of the fast rate of speed that is used to create chenille, the yarn has a tendency to have excess twist. Chenille is steamed after it is created to release the twist, yet not all of the twist can be released. As a result, chenille can loop or "worm" after it is knit. In addition, there is rarely any resilience to chenille, so you must knit it on a needle size much smaller than you would expect from the thickness of the yarn. Most chenille yarns are created with predyed filament fibers so that once the yarn is steamed and dried, it is ready to be knit. The more the yarn is wound, dyed, twisted, and touched, the more chance it has for problems. Some of these problems can be reduced by careful stitch selection. We have found that there are fewer problems when chenille is knit in garter or rib stitch, again on small needles. Any stitch that combines knits and purls in the same row will help control biasing, where the yarn appears to be knit on a slant.

COMPONENT YARNS

THESE ARE SOME of our favorite types of yarns. Many of the yarns we offer are combinations of different strands of fibers and textures put together and twisted, blended, or bound to create a new yarn. Each strand used is considered a component. Textured components can be lashes, flags, puffs, nubs, or spikes.

Any yarn that is generally blended with another yarn can be considered a component. Many of these components are sold separately for you to combine as you please, enabling you to understand what we do when we design a yarn. When working with components, try a variety of things. Combine different base yarns with a variety of components. Try working with each combination in different stitches. Once again, garter and reverse stockinette stitches work well, allowing the textures to stand out.

Component yarns are made on an industrial weaving loom that has hundreds of small hooks on a flat bed. Each hook creates a chain, and the desired texture of the component is injected by a high-speed spindle that is shot back and forth through the chain and locked in place. In some cases, the component yarn is made of raw or undyed fiber. In other cases, depending on the fibers being used, the manufacturer may use undyed and dyed fiber to create a different look. Component yarns are usually made with nylon, viscose, polyester, acetate, and metallic because these fibers dye with brilliance and are strong and easily manipulated.

When designing with component yarns, the texture should be prominent. You can get an idea of how the yarns will work by twisting the component and the base

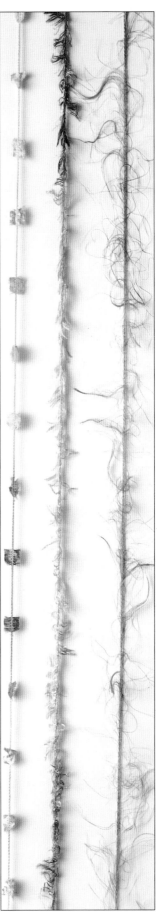

yarns together in circular fashion. Examine what stands out. Do you like the blending of the colors? If the component is space dyed or multicolored, is the base color allowing the component colors to show? Are the textures pleasing together, or do they clash?

In recent years, we have begun using component yarns on their own without blending them. You must either go to a very small needle in order to knit the component like a fabric, or use a medium-size needle and allow the component to be open and lacy. When using component yarns alone, select stitches that feature the texture of the yarn, and keep the design styles very simple.

Eyelash Yarns

EYELASH IS ONE type of component yarn, where long, thread-thin fibers are injected into the chain. A variation of an eyelash yarn is a "flag" component, where shorter fibers are grouped in a square. All of the eyelash-style yarns are made on a loom that chains a base yarn with the lash fiber injected through. The length of the lash varies, depending on the length of time the chain is made without injecting the lash fiber; the lashes are carried alongside the chain and later cut, so a longer interval makes a longer lash. Eyelash yarns can be made of any type of fiber but are most often found in polyester because it is light. Thin strands of polyester are blended, and

when the end of the eyelash is cut, the many plies of polyester bloom open.

Garter and reverse stockinette stitches are recommended because lashes have a tendency to go to the purl side. When using these yarns in slip-stitch patterns, be careful not to select a pattern with a small multiple because the texture of the eyelash and flag yarns will obscure the stitch work. It is unnecessary to pull all of the hairs through to the outside, although some knitters do. Enough texture will show if you ignore the lashes as you knit and allow them to fall naturally. When experimenting with needle size, try larger needles since the lashes and flags will fill in the open spaces around each stitch.

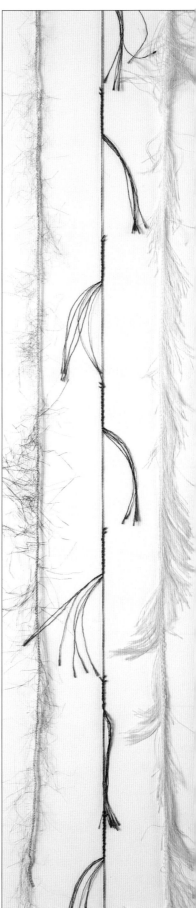

Nub Yarns

Nub yarns are very exciting and are some of the most timeless. A nub is created when a yarn is twisted and pulled through rollers on a twisting machine. The yarn is twisted as it is pulled, and when the pulling stops but the twisting continues, a nub is created. Depending on the length of time that the pulling stops and how slowly the pulling starts again, the nub can be big and full or narrow and long. A binder, usually nylon, is then twisted to secure the effect.

A nub yarn is also called a slub yarn or bump yarn. The nub can be blended with any base fiber, such as cotton, wool, alpaca, acrylic, and more. The effect is twisted to the base yarn so that the nub sits on top of the base, giving depth to the yarn. When knit, the nubs tend to go to the purl side. Good stitches for nub yarns are reverse stockinette and garter. Use a smaller needle when working with nub yarns because they have a tendency to knit too loosely, and you want the stitches to sit close together.

PLIED YARNS

A plied yarn consists of many different strands of yarn placed together. The different yarns, or plies, can be of various fibers. The plies can be run parallel (side by side) or twisted. When plies run parallel, the yarn is more loosely constructed and gives a rustic, homespun look; plies that are twisted are stronger and smoother when knit. The plies themselves can be twisted loosely or tightly. The twists of the plies often run in the opposite direction of the twist of the final yarn. Yarn that is twisted too tightly will bias, or knit on a slant. Multicolored plies give a tweedy effect when knitted. Most classic yarns such as standard knitting worsted are plied. Components used

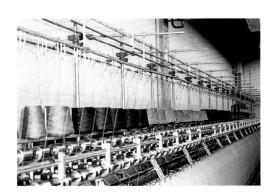

with a base yarn become plied yarns. Find a classic yarn, open the ends, and look at the plies. See if the plies have also been plied, which im-proves strength and resilience.

Plied yarns are versatile and fun to work with because they can be used for every type of knitting. Many different textured stitches work well with plied yarns, and they are often the yarn of choice to show off intricate color and pattern work. The fibers and textures used in the plies and the final thickness of the yarn will determine needle size.

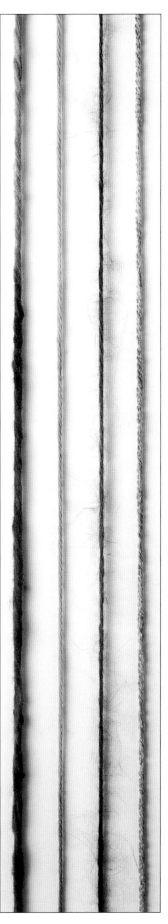

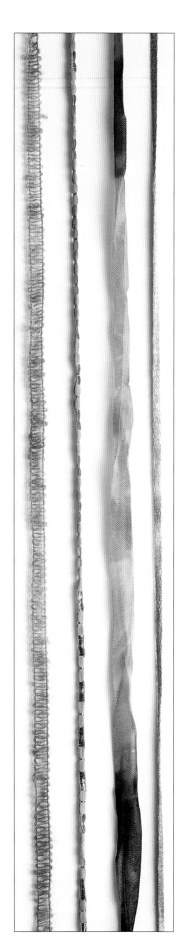

WOVEN YARNS

Woven yarns, or ribbons, are made on a modified weaving loom. The base of the machine is similar to a knitting machine: a flat bed with very small needles lined up. The width of a ribbon depends on the number of needles used. The more needles, the wider the ribbon. Examine the end of a woven ribbon and start to pull the horizontal fiber. The horizontal fiber will pull out, and you will see the vertical fibers set free.

Woven ribbons are versatile, and many variations of stitches and needle sizes can be used successfully. With bigger needles, the woven ribbon remains wide and flat, producing a lighter-weight, draped fabric. With smaller needles, the ribbon folds and creates a crimped look, becoming denser, stiffer, and heavier. Stitch patterns that involve knits and purls, long slipped stitches, loose dropped stitches, and crossed stitches look great because they allow the characteristics of the ribbon to show.

While most woven yarns have a flat appearance, there is no need to keep the yarn flat while knitting. Simply knit as you would any yarn, and the ribbon will curl naturally into the stitch shape. If you wish to minimize the twisting of ribbon, follow the suggestion in the packaging section (page 55).

Stitch Guide

The previous section on yarn types suggests a variety of stitches that work to enhance both the look and the feel of different novelty yarns. This stitch guide explores some of the simpler stitches. Each stitch is illustrated with four swatches, showing the difference in appearance as the yarn type changes. A good stitch dictionary will provide you with many more stitches for your repertoire. Note that any stitch with purl bumps on the right side (reverse stockinette, garter, and seed) makes a nub or a hair more noticeable. Each swatch indicates the type of yarn as well as the pattern stitch.

Once you find a pattern stitch that shows off your yarn well, you can change most basic patterns to use the new stitch. The gauge must be the same, and the total number of stitches on a body piece should equal the multiple of stitches plus any edge stitches. (See pages 54–55 for an explanation of multiples.) Divide the number of stitches for the body by the multiple, round off as necessary, then add any extra edge stitches. For example, let's say you want to use a pattern that is a multiple of 4 plus 2, and 100 stitches are cast on. Since 100 divides evenly by 4, you need to either add 2 stitches or subtract 2 stitches to account for the "plus 2" of the pattern stitch. If you subtract 2 stitches, you would cast on 98 stitches. This results in 96 stitches for the multiple-of-4 pattern, plus 2 edge stitches. If you add 2 stitches, you would cast on 102 stitches. This results in 100 stitches for the multiple of 4, plus 2 edge stitches. You can use your own judgment to determine whether you want the body to be a tiny bit larger or a tiny bit smaller.

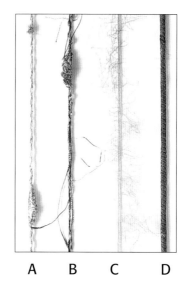

A   B   C   D

STOCKINETTE STITCH

Row 1 (RS): Knit across.
Row 2: Purl across.
Repeat rows 1 and 2.

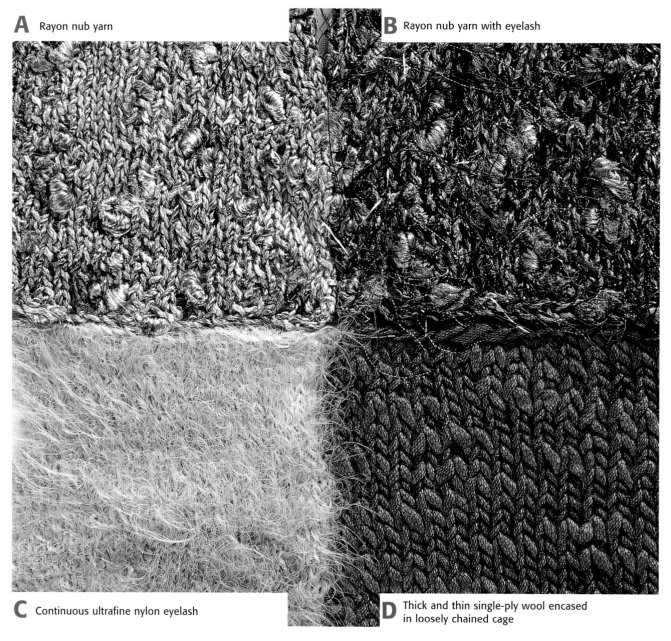

A Rayon nub yarn

B Rayon nub yarn with eyelash

C Continuous ultrafine nylon eyelash

D Thick and thin single-ply wool encased in loosely chained cage

REVERSE STOCKINETTE STITCH

Row 1 (RS): Purl across.
Row 2: Knit across.
Repeat rows 1 and 2.

Notice how the bumps and hairs show up much more on the reverse side.

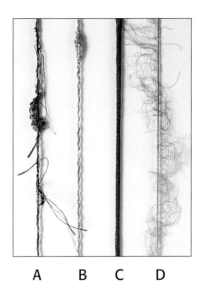

A B C D

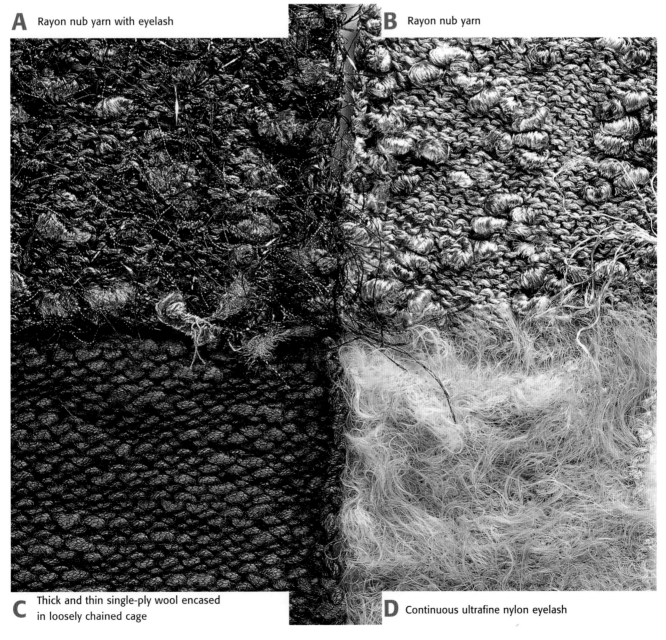

A Rayon nub yarn with eyelash

B Rayon nub yarn

C Thick and thin single-ply wool encased
in loosely chained cage

D Continuous ultrafine nylon eyelash

A   B   C   D

GARTER STITCH

Knit every row.

Garter is easy to do and is a compromise between stockinette and reverse stockinette. It is also reversible, making it ideal for shawls and scarves. The garter stitch tends to stretch in length.

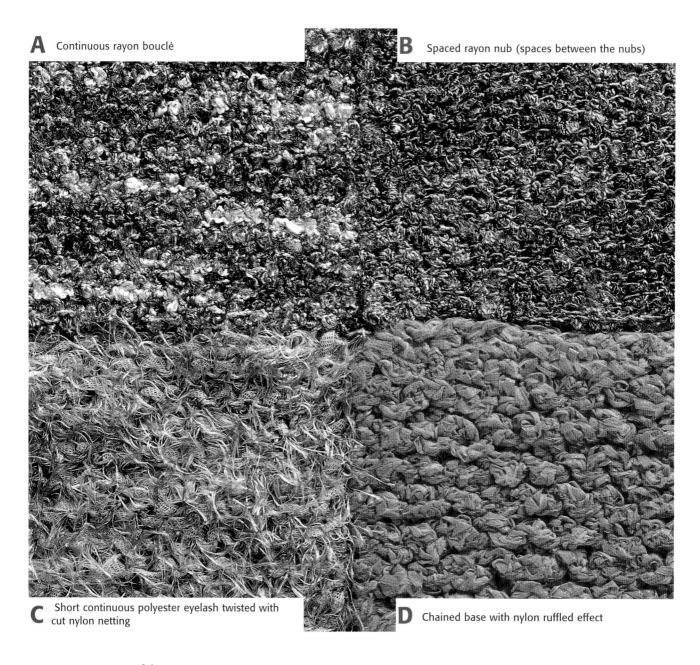

A Continuous rayon bouclé

B Spaced rayon nub (spaces between the nubs)

C Short continuous polyester eyelash twisted with cut nylon netting

D Chained base with nylon ruffled effect

SEED OR MOSS STITCH
(odd number of stitches)

Every row: *K1, P1*; rep from * to *, end K1.

This pattern stitch is also reversible and is somewhat more interesting than garter, although highly textured yarns appear very similar, and seed stitch is slower to make than garter.

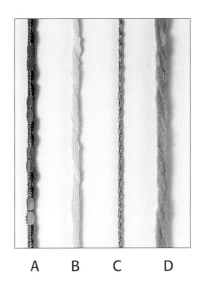

A   B   C   D

A Unspun nylon strands encased in rayon interrupted cage

B Plied cotton with latex component

C Rayon and nylon chainette

D Lightly plied wool and nylon blend

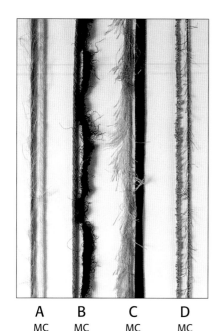

A	B	C	D
MC	MC	MC	MC
+	+	+	+
CC	CC	CC	CC

SIMPLE SLIP STITCH
(multiple of 4; MC is main color)

NOTE: *Slip all stitches purlwise.*

Row 1 (RS): With MC, knit across.
Row 2: With MC, purl across.
Row 3: With CC, K1, *sl 1 wyib, K3*; rep from * to *, end sl 1 wyib, K2.
Row 4: With CC, P2, *sl 1 wyif, P3*; rep from * to *, end sl 1 wyif, P1.
Row 5: With MC, knit across.
Row 6: With MC, purl across.
Row 7: With CC, K3, *sl 1 wyib, K3*; rep from * to *, end K1.
Row 8: With CC, P4, *sl 1 wyif, P3*; rep from * to *.
Repeat rows 1–8.

You will use about 20 to 25 percent more of color A, since every stitch is worked, while B is only worked in three-fourths of the stitches and the rest are slipped. A flat background pops the textured yarn off the surface. When reversed, the texture is punctuated with small, flat dots.

A Lightly spun nylon twisted with soft nylon eyelash (MC); plied wool (CC)

B Plied wool (MC); chained base with nylon frill and eyelash effects (CC)

C Continuous long nylon eyelash (MC); knitted rayon tape (CC)

D Continuous nub rayon (CC); short nylon eyelash (CC)

Tweed Checks
(multiple of 10 plus 9)

NOTE: *Slip all stitches purlwise.*

Rows 1 and 3 (RS): With MC, knit across.

Rows 2 and 4: With MC, purl across.

Row 5: With CC, K1, sl 1 wyib, K1, sl 3 wyib, *(K1, sl 1 wyib) 3 times, K1, sl 3 wyib; rep from * to last 3 sts, K1, sl 1 wyib, K1.

Row 6: With CC, K1, sl 1 wyif, K1, sl 3 wyif, *(K1, sl 1 wyif) 3 times, K1, sl 3 wyif; rep from * to last 3 sts, K1, sl 1 wyif, K1.

Row 7: With MC, knit across.

Row 8: With MC, purl across.

Repeat rows 5–8 twice more, then repeat rows 5 and 6 again.

Repeat these 18 rows.

This stitch is great for playing a textured yarn against a flat yarn. The nubby garter stitches that are separated by the plain yarn really pop off the surface. The repeat is large, so you may have to do some calculations to substitute this into an existing pattern.

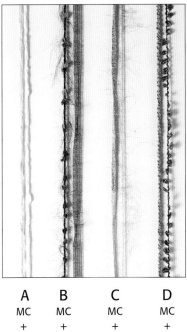

A	B	C	D
MC	MC	MC	MC
+	+	+	+
CC	CC	CC	CC

A Plied cotton with latex component, 2 different colors (MC=white, CC=yellow)

B Nylon-blend eyelash twisted with nylon pompon (MC); cotton/nylon blend woven tape (CC)

C Woven rayon ribbon (MC); continuous shiny nylon eyelash (CC)

D Crepe twist cotton (MC); continuous rayon bouclé (CC)

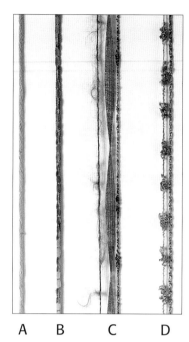

A   B   C   D

LINEN STITCH
(odd number of stitches)

NOTE: *Slip all stitches purlwise.*

Row 1: *K1, sl 1 wyif*; rep from * to *, end K1.
Row 2: P2, *sl 1 wyib, P1*; rep from * to *, end P1.
Repeat rows 1 and 2.

You must use a much larger needle than you think, since this stitch compresses quite a bit. For example, if a size 8 is called for, try an 11. This is a great stitch for blending more than one color of yarn, since the rows are drawn into each other. Try alternating 2 rows each of many different colors and textures, or choose 3 yarns and work 1 row of each for maximum blending.

TIP: *After knitting any slip stitch, grasp the top and bottom edges of the knitting and pull firmly from top to bottom. Then grasp the sides and pull gently from side to side, which helps to "set" the stitches and gives a more even look to the fabric.*

A Plied cotton

B Unplied nylon strands encased in interrupted rayon cage

C Two rows woven cotton/polyester tape alternated with two rows mohair and metallic mix

D Two rows chained rayon and nylon alternated with two rows rayon nub

HALF LINEN STITCH
(odd number of stitches)

NOTE: *Slip all stitches purlwise.*

Row 1: *K1, sl 1 wyif*; rep from * to *, end K1.
Row 2: Purl across.
Row 3: K2, *sl 1 wyif, K1*; rep from * to *, end K1.
Row 4: Purl across.
Repeat rows 1–4.

Half linen stitch (so called because you only work the slips on half of the rows) does not compress as much as linen stitch and doesn't take as much time to work since you only slip on half the rows. Use a larger than normal needle, but not as large as for the linen stitch. For example, if a size 8 is called for, try a 10.

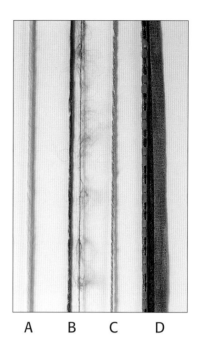

A　B　C　D

A Plied wool

B Kid mohair/rayon single-ply blend

C Cotton plied with interrupted short polyester-blend eyelash, 3 different colors, alternated, 1 row each

D Knitted rayon tape, woven rayon ribbon, and stranded nylon with interrupted rayon cage, alternated, 1 row each

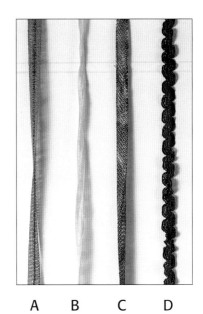

A   B   C   D

DROPPED LONG STITCH

Row 1 (RS): Knit across.
Row 2: Knit across.
Row 3: Knit across, wrapping yarn around needle twice for each stitch.
Row 4: Knit across, dropping extra loops from needle.
Repeat rows 1–4.

This stitch is particularly beautiful for ribbons and tapes, where you wish to see as much of the actual yarn itself as possible. You may use the dropped stitch as an allover texture, or you can use it as an accent separated by bands of stockinette or garter stitch.

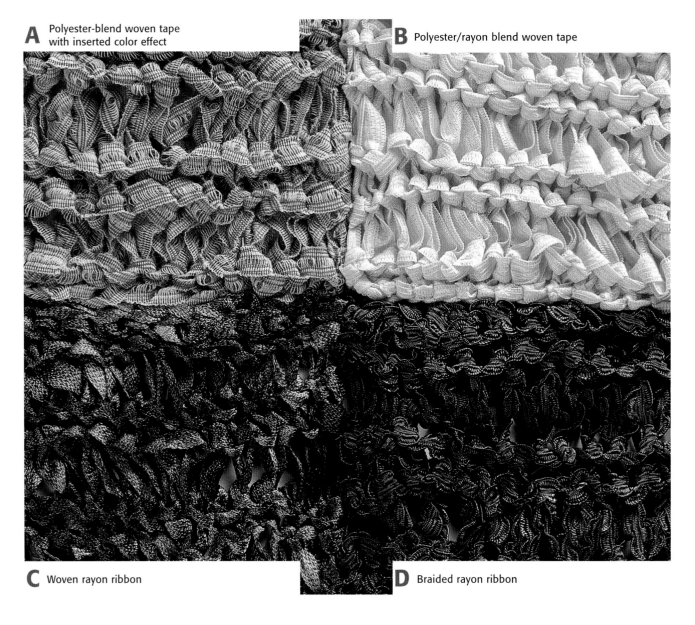

A Polyester-blend woven tape with inserted color effect

B Polyester/rayon blend woven tape

C Woven rayon ribbon

D Braided rayon ribbon

DROPPED CABLE STITCH
(multiple of 4 plus 2)

Row 1 (RS): Knit across.

Row 2: Knit across.

Row 3: Knit across, wrapping yarn around needle twice for each stitch.

Row 4: K1, *sl next 2 sts to cable needle and hold in front, dropping extra
loops from needle; knit next 2 sts, dropping extra loops from needle,
K2 sts from cable needle*; rep from * to *, end K1.

Repeat rows 1–4.

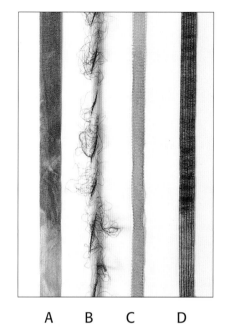

A   B   C   D

Anything you can do with regular knitting you can also do with long stitches—although not everything looks as good as this! You can also elongate the stitches even more by wrapping three times around the needle, and you can cross any number of stitches that you wish. You can make waves by wrapping once, then twice, then three times and back down again, as Barry has done in his wrap, "Waves of Pleasure" on page 122.

A ½"-wide woven rayon ribbon

B Single-ply acrylic wrapped with continuous nylon eyelash

C Cut nylon netting

D Polyester/rayon woven ribbon

BLUEPRINT FOR FIT

A MAJOR CAUSE OF what we call "ill-fitting syndrome" is the fact that there is no standard of fit for knitting patterns. Designers draw patterns to their own preference in fit, with the amount of ease they like, so it's a good idea to consider patterns as *suggested* dimensions. A medium in ready-to-wear doesn't necessarily translate to a given designer's medium in a knitting pattern, just as sewing-pattern sizing differs wildly from ready-to-wear. Forethought, planning, and knowing your proper measurements will add greatly to the increased success of your knitting.

Taking Accurate Measurements

The first thing necessary to guarantee fit is an accurate set of measurements. The chart below lists measurements that we consider crucial for proper fit. With a partner to help, record the following:

CORE BODY MEASUREMENTS

Bust or chest: measure around fullest part, making sure tape measure is level

Waist: measure at narrowest part

Hips: measure around fullest part

Arm length: measure from shoulder bone to wrist bone

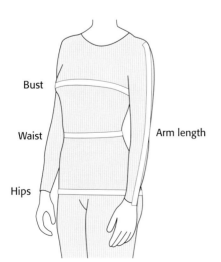

Shoulder: measure straight across back from bone to bone

Back neck length: measure from back neck bone to waist

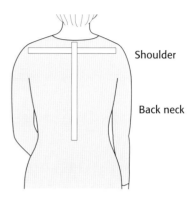

Upper arm: measure around arm at widest point above elbow, with arm extended

Arm depth: Hold straight needle firmly under arm as shown; measure from top of shoulder bone down front to needle under arm (a) for front-to-shoulder measurement. Measure from needle in back, up over shoulder, to needle in front for total front-to-back arm depth (b).

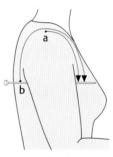

a: arm depth
b: total arm depth

Additionally, stand straight and tall before a mirror and look at your shoulders. Many patterns have straight shoulders, and if your shoulders slope, this can lead to poor fit. Slope can easily be built into any pattern by taking the number of stitches for each shoulder and binding them off in steps from the armhole toward the neck, instead of all at once. The smaller the steps, the more slope you will build in. Slope keeps the knitting from stretching and straining around the neck area and is more important in close-fitting garments.

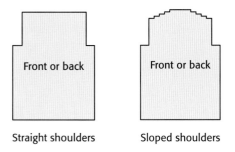

Straight shoulders   Sloped shoulders

Customizing Patterns

ALLOWING FOR EASE

Before a pattern can be checked for fit, you need to know one more important thing: how much ease you personally want. Analyze the style of the garment and the hand of the yarn when deciding on ease. Typically, outer garments will need more ease than dressier, fitted garments. Coats, jackets, and cardigans must have enough ease for normal clothing to be worn under them. Equally important is the type of yarn selected. Heavier, stiffer yarns produce fabric that stands away from the body. If too much ease is added, visual bulk is added to the wearer.

Very soft yarns that drape can have more ease built in, since they tend to cling and you may not want body definition. Sweaters that will be worn under jackets or coats must not have so much ease that they do not fit comfortably under the outer garment, particularly in the upper sleeve width and the depth of armhole.

Using a garment from your closet whose fit you like, take the same measurements on the garment that you took from your body. For truly custom fitting, do this for several garments: one that is closely fitted, one that is average fit, and one that is oversized. We design with a bust measurement equal to one's own bust measurement for fitted garments, about 2" larger for average fit, and about 5" larger for oversized. We know some who like up to 10" of ease for every sweater they make!

This is the information needed to create a blueprint for fit. After you select a pattern, decide which category the garment is in: close, average, or oversized. Turn to the pattern diagram. Compare the width measurements with the measurement from the garment whose fit you like. Forget what the designer's designation is. Select the size that is based on the width/ease measurement. This will give you the base numbers to start with, but there are other things you need to check in the pattern.

Compare your bust and hip measurement. Generally you will make the size that fits the larger measurement. The tendency when selecting a sweater size is to go by bust measurement, but if the sweater style is long enough to cover the hips, the size should be selected with hip ease in mind. For many, that is a larger measurement than the bust. If the reverse is true, then pick your size based on the bust measurement. In any event, pick the size based on the larger number. The exception is for cropped sweaters or those that hit the high-hip area; they do not need to accommodate the hips.

The most critical fitting point after overall ease is the shoulder width, which often has nothing to do with girth. Large people can have narrow shoulders; small people can have wide shoulders. Patterns are written for some unknown average—not for you or me! Garments with set-in sleeves whose sleeve-to-body seam drops below the shoulder bone have an incorrect fit and look sloppy. If your shoulders are narrow compared to the rest of you and the sweater has a dropped shoulder, the armhole seam may be halfway down the arm! The solution is a careful auditing of the pattern for shoulder width. Check the shoulders after armhole shaping. If the diagram does not show this measurement, calculate it by taking the number of stitches left after any armhole shaping and dividing that number by the stitch gauge. The total width should be smaller than your actual shoulder measurement if the sleeve is set in, about your measurement for a modified drop shoulder (one where the body cuts straight in at the armholes), and only an inch or two below the shoulder for a casual look. You may find that you have to lose substantially more stitches during the armhole shaping than the pattern calls for to get the sleeve-to-body seam in the right place.

Correct fit
for shoulders

Incorrect fit
for shoulders

Compare the armhole depth of the pattern with your actual armhole depth. Laura likes her close-fitting sweaters with about 1" added to the depth; average fit, about 1½" to 2"; and oversized drop shoulder, up to 4". Set-in sleeves should be closer fitting—if the armhole is too deep, the sleeves and body pull up when you move. Drop-shoulder and modified drop-shoulder sleeves require more ease, since there is no underarm shaping. Compare these measurements with the ones from your favorite garment. Make any adjustments in depth.

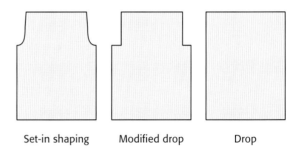

Set-in shaping   Modified drop   Drop

ADJUSTING SLEEVE LENGTH

The last fitting point is sleeve length. Traditional garments with tight cuffs tend to hide any stretching over time: the sleeve merely blouses above the cuff. More modern styles, often with straight sleeve bottoms, show every bit of stretch. When the body of a garment stretches, it gets longer and is not a serious problem; when sleeves stretch, they become annoying. Sometimes sleeves can be shortened by simply reinforcing the shoulder seam to pull it in and the sleeves up—a much easier fix than re-knitting. Best of all is to get it right the first time.

The arm length is for a sleeve's total length. For a set-in sleeve, subtract 3" (a constant to allow for sleeve-cap shaping) from the armhole depth of the sweater, and then subtract this new number from the sleeve length. This is the length you need to the underarm. For a drop shoulder or modified-drop inset, locate where on the shoulder or upper arm the edge of the sweater body will hit. If it is not right on top of the shoulder at the edge of the arm, then you need to subtract from the total sleeve length however much the body drops down. Knit the sleeve to within 1" to 2" of the underarm (set-in sleeve) or total (other types of sleeves) length. Leave the sleeve on the needle. Hang a pillowcase over a hanger, and pin the sleeve to the pillowcase with T-pins, along the needle. Hang overnight or longer if you have the time. This will "prestretch" the sleeve, giving a more accurate measurement, and is particularly useful with heavier novelty yarns that tend to stretch over time. Check the measurement of the sleeve.

NOTE: *Always hold your knitting upright when measuring the sleeves and body lengths, to mimic how the knitted garment will act when it is worn.*

Finish knitting the sleeve, making any adjustments to length. If the yarn is heavy or particularly stretchy, you may have to rip back some rows.

Custom–Fit Techniques

DIFFERENT HIP AND BUST SIZES

One of the easiest fixes you can make to customize fit involves determining your hip-to-bust ratio. If you are one of the many women whose hips are more than 4" different from their bust, then this section is for you—whether you are larger in the hip or in the bust!

If your hips are the wider measurement, then the danger when allowing enough ease to accommodate the hips (especially in a longer sweater) is that once the knitting gets to the armhole shaping, there is far too much fabric around the bust. This makes it difficult to do smooth armhole shaping and leads to too much fabric and bulk around the underarms. The solution is to taper the sweater from hem to armhole. Relatively little taper over the length of the body will accomplish better fit without disrupting the look of the garment. For example, for a 42" hip with 6" of ease allowed and a bust of 38" with a desired ease of 3", the sweater body piece would need to be 24" at the hem and taper to 20½" at the bust. Since most sweaters designed to accommodate that much ease over the hip are longer sweaters, the body length is probably at least 16" to the armhole. Removing approximately 1½" from each side seam over a length of 16" will accomplish the goal. If the stitch gauge is 5 stitches per inch, decrease 8 times on each side seam, one stitch for every 2". If the row gauge is a typical 7 or 8 stitches per inch for that stitch gauge, decreasing once every 14 or 16 rows will be sufficient. This will never be noticed at the side seam and is even easy to work into pattern stitches or color work. For paneled pattern stitches, such as Aran-style sweaters, simply leave enough of the edge stitches in seed stitch to allow for the decreasing. For color work or allover patterns, work the remaining stitches in pattern as far as possible.

Body taper
Hips larger than bust

The more unusual body type where the bust is 4" or more larger than the hip measurement produces a sweater stretched tight over the bust or a sweater that accommodates the bust and flaps around loosely at the hip or waist. This is especially pronounced if the sweater is cropped to the waist or high hip. The solution here is to do the opposite of the above: start with fewer stitches at the bottom and increase gradually toward the armhole. Since often a large bust measurement is unequally divided between the front and back, increasing on the front more than the back makes sense. Some increasing on the back will be helpful in making the two body pieces more closely match visually, but you can do twice as much increasing on the front. Once you get to the armhole shaping, bind off more and decrease more on the front to bring the shoulder to the same measurement as the back. This should be done gradually—you don't want a huge curve cutting in right at the bust level, but a gentle taper all the way up the armhole edge until the shoulder is reached.

Body taper
Bust larger than hips

CREEPING BACK AND FRONT

One of the most common problems we see is a sweater whose hem rides up in either the front or back: in the front, it's usually due to large busts on women or potbellies on men; in the back, it's often due to rounded backs that occur typically in women as they age. In either case, a piece that rides up needs to have extra material built in, without disrupting the pattern and while still having the front and back work together visually. Often, but not always, this is done with short rows, working extra rows in the middle of the piece, but not going all the way to the edge so the edges still match.

Creeping Back

This problem is easy to fix and can generally be done without short rows, unless the rounded back is very pronounced. Often, all of the extra material can be added between the underarm and the shoulder, where it will not show at all unless there are matching stripes between the sleeve and the body.

Using the measurements taken earlier in this section, compare the top of shoulder to underarm (a) with the total front to back (b). If the front-to-shoulder number is less than one-half of the total, then you can lengthen the armhole depth on the back to accommodate the difference. This adds more actual fabric to the back, in the upper area where the rounding usually occurs, and allows the shoulder seam to sit in the proper place on top of the shoulders. Unless there is a radical difference, the setting in of the sleeve will not be affected. Adjust the sleeve-cap length to allow for the extra fabric: when figuring the sleeve-cap depth, add one-half the amount you have added in the back to the total cap depth. Center the sleeve in the armhole, easing the extra depth toward the back. For a drop or T-inset sleeve, simply center the sleeve.

Creeping Front

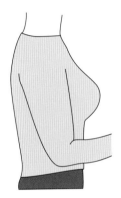

The theory for correcting a creeping front is the same as for the back: more fabric is needed in the front piece between the hem and the top. For a pot-belly, you can work the extra rows throughout the body from hem to underarm, as spread out as possible. If the pattern has intricate color work or pattern stitches, keep several edge stitches in something plain that can be matched to the back. If the ease is for a large bust, center the extra rows across the bust area, typically beginning about 4" to 6" below the underarm. If you have intricate color or pattern work, you can build in some ease by reversing the armhole trick and making the front armhole depth longer than the back.

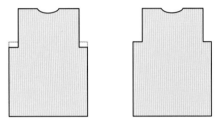

Make front or back longer in armhole
as necessary to correct creep.

KNITTING SUCCESSFULLY WITH NOVELTY YARNS

Gauge: How to Get It Right

A gauge swatch should always be made before proceeding with a project. Please remember that even though you may think you are always "on gauge," you don't know that the pattern writer is! To avoid tears later, always check before you start, and check every few inches as you knit. Even the most experienced knitters have had a gauge change on them when they move from a swatch to a garment.

Cast on enough stitches to make 4", for example, at 4½ sts per inch, cast on 18 sts. Knit 3" to 4", working in the pattern stitch. Without binding off, slip the swatch off the needle. With a flat ruler, not a tape measure, measure on the purl side of the swatch, flattening it at the edges with the ruler. If it is larger than 4", try a smaller needle size (go down two sizes if it is much bigger); if it is smaller, go up in size. Make another swatch with the new needle size, and repeat until you get exactly 4".

Count the row gauge at this point and compare it to the pattern row gauge. If your row gauge is tighter, that is, more rows per inch than the pattern, you will need more yarn; if looser, you will need less yarn.

Bind off and save your gauge swatch. You can use it if you need extra yarn to finish, as repair yarn, and as a record. Attach a label from the yarn to your swatch, and record needle size and gauge. You may also use the swatch to see how the yarn will behave during laundering.

Dye Lots

In an ideal world, we would purchase enough yarn of the same lot to complete our garment, but sometimes we do run short. If the dye lot is not available, purchase a different lot, then alternate the new yarn with the old for as many inches as you can—a minimum of 6" and an entire piece if possible. Any variations in the new will blend into the old without a line where the two join. When you first begin a project, check to see how much knitting is completed after using one full ball of yarn. You can make a good estimate of how much yarn you will need, and purchase more, if necessary, before you continue.

Label Information

The label on yarn contains important information. Save a label for each yarn used, and read the information carefully to plan a successful project. The label for your yarn may contain some or all of the information below.

1. Company name
2. Yarn name
3. Fiber content
4. Weight in grams (g) and/or ounces (oz)
5. Length in yards and/or meters
6. Expected gauge and needle size
7. Color of yarn
8. Dye-lot number
9. Care instructions
10. Country where yarn is manufactured

Front

Back

Metric to English Conversion

Labels list weight in grams or ounces, and yardage in meters or yards, depending on whether they are manufactured in Europe or the United States. Following are the most commonly used measurements and their equivalents:

> 20 g = 0.7 oz.
> 25 g = 0.88 oz.
> 50 g = 1.75 oz.
> 100 g = 3.5 oz.
> Kilo = 1000 g = 2.2 lbs. or 35 oz.
> Yards = meters plus 10 percent; for example,
> 50 m = 55 yds.

Stitch Pattern Repeats and Multiples

When reading a stitch pattern, you will see that each row is written out. It is important to read each line carefully and to understand what it is you are required to do. For successful work, you must follow specific punctuation. Let's look at the following pattern row as an example:

> K2, P4, *K2, YO, sl 1, K1, PSSO*; rep from * to *
> 6 times, end K2.

Work the stitches as stated, paying attention to the stitches between the asterisks (*). These asterisks indicate a series of stitches that you will repeat. Work the stitches once, then repeat them as many times as possible to the end of the row, or a specific number of times if this is indicated; for example, rep from * to * 6 times. Sometimes the directions will include an additional stitch(es) at the end of the row. For example, rep from * to *, end K2 means to repeat the stitches between the asterisks as many times as needed to cross the row, then end by knitting the last 2 stitches.

To check the multiple, simply count the stitches being worked between the asterisks. In our example, the multiple is 4.

To know how many stitches to cast on, you need to know the multiple plus any other stitches asked for in the stitch pattern. In our example, we have a repeat of 4 plus 8 stitches. You could cast on 12 stitches, 28 stitches, or 48 stitches as each is a multiple of 4 plus 8.

Slip Stitches

When working a slip-stitch pattern, it is important to remember the following:

- When you see wyib (with yarn in back), put yarn in the back of your work as if you are knitting, before slipping the stitch(es).

- When you see wyif (with yarn in front), put yarn in the front of your work as if you are purling, before slipping the stitch(es).

- Always slip the stitch(es) as if you are purling them unless the pattern states differently. This will transfer the stitch(es) from one needle to the other without twisting them.

Packaging

The packaging of yarns varies from company to company and with yarn type. Each company selects a style of packaging that will best enhance the appearance of the yarn. The following covers most forms of packaging, with hints on how to manage the yarn.

Balls: Remove the label and keep it as a reference. Find the outside end of the yarn, or carefully reach into the middle of the ball and look for the inside end to use as a pull skein. Yarn from a pull skein, one from the manufacturer or one you wind yourself on a ball winder, has a twist added to it by the act of winding. Most of the time this isn't noticeable, but with ribbons, extra twists can be annoying. To minimize twisting, place a straight knitting needle through the center of the ball or spool, hold the needle horizontally, and gently pull on the yarn from the outside. The ball will rotate around the needle, and the yarn or ribbon will feed off without an added twist.

Cones: Simply pull from the outside and work. To keep from adding extra twists, we recommend that you make the cone swivel by using the needle trick from above, or by placing the cone on a horizontal spindle.

Hanks: Untwist the hank and have someone hold the hank open between their hands, or place the hank on a swift (a reel for winding yarn). Remove the label and cut any ties. We recommend that you attach the beginning tail to the label and wind the yarn around your fingers and the label to keep the information for later reference. If you have a ball winder, save the label and push it into the center of the ball at the end of winding, or attach it to the tail if you are using the ball as a pull skein.

Creating a Pattern Library

Create a notebook for your own pattern library. For every project that you make, save a piece of the yarn and the label (A). Attach the gauge swatch to the label, and keep everything in a clear-plastic page holder. To make a permanent record of the needle size on your gauge swatch, work *YO, K2tog* for each number in the needle size. For example, on size 7 needle, work the openwork pattern 7 times a few rows before binding off. This will give you a row of lace with 7 holes that you can count later so you know what your gauge was on a size 7 needle (B). Another alternative is to put a knot in the tail for each number in the needle size (C). Or, it may be easier to attach a label to each swatch and write down the important information.

Weaving in Ends

Many sweaters never get finished because of those pesky ends! To minimize the clean-up chore at the end of a project, get into the habit of weaving them in as you go. Carry the yarn ends across the back, in and out of the working yarn. When you're a few rows away, tug the knitting gently from side to side to make sure the ends aren't distorting your work.

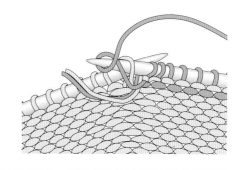

TIP

To help with sewing seams, leave a very long end when you cast on. The end can be used for seaming, and there is one less end to weave in!

TRENDSETTER
YARNS
DUNE
41% MOH
12% VISCO
6% METAL

TRENDSETTER
YARNS
APROPOS
68 % SI
18 % MO
Needles #

Care Instructions

Many yarn labels recommend dry cleaning. They say this because the manufacturers are not able to go home with you to ensure that the knits are handled properly. See below for a description of symbols used on yarn labels.

In general, it is safe to hand wash hand knits. Do this in a clean, shallow sink. Do not use bleach in the sink before washing your knit because residual bleach can harm the garment. Use a mild soap specifically made for knitwear, white dishwashing liquid, or baby soap. Dissolve the soap in lukewarm water and gently add the knitted garment. Press down, allowing the water to flow through. Do not twist and turn the knit as this will stretch it, but press up and down gently. After a moment or so, let the water run out of the sink. Set the stopper again, push the knit aside, and fill the sink with water at the same temperature as before. Push down on the knit several times to remove the soap. After emptying the sink on the last rinse, push down on the knit to remove as much water as possible. Gently pull the knitted garment into a ball and place it on a dry towel or flat sweater rack. Open up the garment and position it to dry so that it does not stretch or grow. You may place it in a lingerie bag and in the washer on the spin cycle to spin out excess water. Make sure it is on spin only, with no agitation and no water coming in. Never put a wet knit on a hanger.

If you are concerned about the dye bleeding or how the yarn will respond to washing, save your knit swatch and experiment. It is better to find out early what the constraints of a yarn are so that when you are done, you have a knit that fits, is done beautifully, and can be cared for properly.

The following symbols are used to provide information on the care of your yarn.

Washing

	Do not wash
	Hand wash in warm water
	Hand wash at stated temperature
	Machine wash
	Do not tumble dry
	Tumble drying OK
	Dry flat
	No bleach
	Chlorine bleach OK

Pressing

	Do not iron
	Cool iron
	Warm iron
	Hot iron

Dry Cleaning Symbols

	Do not dry clean
	Dry cleanable in all solvents
	Dry cleanable with fluorocarbon or petroleum-based solvents only
	Dry cleanable with perchlorethylene, hydrocarbons, or a petroleum-based solvent

THE FLOCK EXCHANGE

When we set out to write this book, we felt it was important to show how different types of yarns and textures can make a design take on a new look. To accomplish this, we each designed original sweaters. Then we exchanged patterns and reinterpreted each other's designs. In some cases the yarns alone made a difference, while at other times a simple style change was made, such as turning a pullover into a cardigan. The following projects feature photographs of each style and take you through our thought processes for both the original designs and the variations. We hope that this information will inspire you to make your own flock exchange: swatch, experiment, be creative, and have fun—we did!

MULTIYARN MAGIC

Designed by Barry Klein

BARRY'S VERSION (OPPOSITE): There are times a designer puts yarns, colors, and stitches together, and it just works. This sweater did that for me. In swatching the yarns, I found they all blended the way my eye wanted them to. By playing with a few stitches, the differences in the true gauges of each yarn became unimportant. I just love this sweater and believe that it can be made for a man as well.

LAURA'S VERSION (ABOVE): I was amazed at how beautiful Barry's combinations are. I had never considered using wide bands of different yarns because of the different hands and gauges they each have. With this concept as inspiration, I made the same sweater with a selection of Prism yarns, and I am equally amazed at how beautiful my version is. One is never too old to learn new tricks!

Barry's Version

SIZES

Small (Medium, Large, X-Large, XX-Large)

KNITTED MEASUREMENTS

(approx.)

Bust: 34 (38, 42, 46, 50)"

MATERIALS

Trendsetter Yarns

(A) 4 (4, 4, 5, 5) balls Dune (50g/90yds), color #85

(B) 1 (1, 1, 1, 1) ball Balboa (50g/150yds), color #105

(C) 1 (1, 1, 1, 1) ball Balboa, color #23

(D) 1 (1, 1, 1, 2) balls Sunshine (50g/95yds), color #35

(E) 2 (2, 2, 3, 3) balls Charm (20g/90yds), color #1001

(F) 2 (2, 2, 2, 3) balls Fresco (50g/75yds), color #603

(G) 2 (2, 2, 2, 3) balls Zucca (50g/72yds), color #707

1 pair each of size 8 US and size 9 US needles, or size to obtain correct gauge

GAUGE

18 sts and 24 rows = 4" in stock st and Dune on size 9 needles

BACK

With size 8 needle and A, CO 80 (88, 96, 104, 112) sts. Work in K2, P2 rib for 2 (2, 3, 3, 3)". Change to size 9 needles and work the following stripe sequence:

Stripe 1: With G, K4, P4 for 6 rows. Your size may not work out to an exact rep. Work sts as possible, and after armhole shaping, adjust alignment.

Stripe 2:

Row 1: *K1 in B, K1 in C*; rep from * to *.

Row 2: P back, working in opposite colors as set.

Stripe 3: *K 2 rows in D, K 2 rows in E*; rep from * to *, 3 times total.

Stripe 4: Rep stripe 2.

Stripe 5: Work A in stock st for 2".

Stripe 6: Rep stripe 2.

Stripe 7: Work F in stock st for 10 rows.

Stripe 8: Rep stripe 2.

Stripe 9: Work A in stock st for 2".

Stripe 10: Rep stripe 2.

Work stripes 1–10, then rep sequence. When 15" from CO or desired length to underarm, BO 8 (9, 10, 11, 12) sts at beg of next 2 rows until 64 (70,76, 82, 88) sts remain. Work even until armhole is 7½ (8, 8½, 8½, 9)". BO rem sts.

FRONT

Work as for back until armhole is 5 (5½, 6, 6½, 7)". BO center 14 sts. Join new yarn and work both neck edges at same time. BO 2 sts at each neck edge once. Dec 1 st at each neck edge every other row 6 times. Cont to same length as back. BO rem sts.

SLEEVES

With size 8 needles and A, CO 30 (32, 32, 34, 36) sts. Work K2, P2 rib for 2 (2, 3, 3, 3)", inc 16 (14, 16, 16, 16) sts evenly across last row. Change to size 9 needles and work in stripe sequence, inc 1 st at each end every 8 (7, 7, 7, 7) rows 11 (13, 13, 13, 14) times and working new sts into patt until you have 68 (72, 74, 76, 80) sts. Work even until sleeve is 18 (18, 18½, 19, 19)" from CO. BO sts loosely.

FINISHING

Sew left shoulder seam. With size 8 needles, beg at back neck, pick up 1 st with B, 1 st with C, alternating around complete neck until 86 (86, 88, 88, 90) sts are on needle. Work in stock st, as for stripe 2 for 2". Change to A and BO. Neck will roll forward. Sew shoulder and neck. Sew sleeves to body. Sew sleeve and side seams.

Laura's Version

MATERIALS

Prism Yarns

(A) 5 (6, 6, 7, 7) skeins Kid Slique (2oz/88yds), color Autumn

(B) 1 (2, 2, 2, 2) skeins Bon Bon (2oz/94yds), color #112 Teal

(C) 1 (2, 2, 2, 2) skeins Bon Bon, color Terra Cotta

(D) 2 (2, 2, 2, 3) skeins Sunshine (1oz/65yds), color Firefox

(E) 2 (2, 2, 3, 3) skeins Twirl (1oz/65yds), color Autumn

(F) 2 (3, 3, 3, 4) skeins Luna (1oz/58yds), color Firefox

(G) 1 (2, 2, 2, 3) skeins Cleo (1.5oz/82yds), color Terra Cotta

1 pair each of size 8 US and size 9 US needles, or size to obtain correct gauge

GAUGE

18 sts and 24 rows = 4" in stock st and Kid Slique on size 9 needles

DIRECTIONS

Work as for Barry's Version, using the yarn substitutions above.

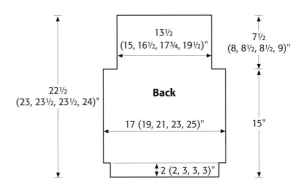

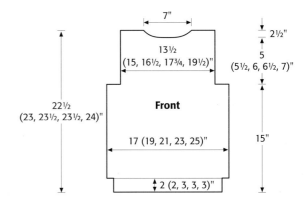

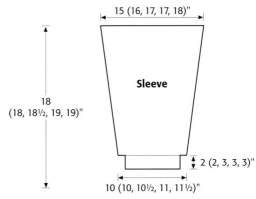

THREE FOR THE ROAD

Designed by Laura Bryant

LAURA'S VERSION (OPPOSITE): I enjoy lifting details from ready-to-wear. This little blouse was inspired by one owned by my office manager. I measured the dimensions on her sweater and wrote these instructions. Neat details include the clever collar, cap sleeve, and tapered body. The pattern stitch is fun to knit, and using three different yarns in one-row stripes is easy and gives a great look. Each yarn is improved by being alternated; the best qualities shine through, the colors blend beautifully, and problems are masked.

BARRY'S VERSION (ABOVE): I think this sweater is so cute and really wearable. My thoughts centered on what would happen with two solid and only one printed color. The swatch showed that the subtle texture and single printed color balanced themselves nicely against the solid background colors. It's a hit!

Laura's Version

SIZES

Small (Medium, Large, X-Large)

KNITTED MEASUREMENTS

(approx.)

Bust: 35 (38, 42, 46)"

MATERIALS

Prism Yarns

(A) 4 (5, 6, 6) skeins Tulle (1oz/96yds), color Tahoe

(B) 5 (6, 7, 9) skeins Biwa (1oz/68yds), color Senegal

(C) 4 (5, 6, 6) skeins Slique (2oz/88yds), color Firefox

1 skein Quicksilver (2oz/160yds), color Autumn

1 pair of size 7 US needles, or size to obtain correct gauge

Size E crochet hook

6 small glass buttons

GAUGE

20 sts and 34 rows = 4" in half linen stitch on size 7 needles

HALF LINEN STITCH

(worked on even number of sts)

Row 1: K1, *sl 1 wyif, K1*; rep from * to *, end K1.

Row 2: Purl across.

Row 3: K1, *K1, sl 1 wyif*; rep from * to *, end K1.

Row 4: Purl across.

Rep rows 1–4.

Color sequence: Work 1 row each with A, B, and C. When a row is complete, the next color you need is waiting.

BACK

With A, CO 80 (90, 100, 110) sts. Beg patt, inc 1 st at each edge every 2" 4 times until there are 88 (98, 108, 118) sts. Work to 11 (11½, 12, 13)" from CO or desired length to underarm. BO 4 (4, 5, 6) sts at beg of next 2 rows. BO 3 sts at beg of next 2 rows. BO 2 sts at beg of next 2 rows. Dec 1 st at each edge every other row 3 times until 64 (74, 82, 90) sts remain. Work even to armhole depth of 7½, (8, 8½, 9)", then shape shoulders: BO 4 (5, 6, 7) sts at beg of next 8 rows. BO rem sts.

LEFT FRONT

With A, CO 44 (48, 54, 60) sts. Work as for back, inc 1 st every 2" at beg of RS rows 4 times until there are 48 (52, 58, 64) sts. Work to 11 (11½, 12, 13)" from CO or desired length to underarm; shape armhole at beg of RS rows only as for back. At the same time, when 12¾ (13½, 14, 15)" from CO, beg lapel shaping, inc 1 st every 6 rows at end of RS rows 5 times. When work is 16½ (17, 17½, 18)" from CO, shape neck: BO 15 sts at beg of next WS row. At same edge, BO 4 sts once, 3 sts once, then dec 1 st at same edge every other row 3 (3, 4, 5) times. At the same time, when same length as back, BO 4 (5, 6, 7) sts at beg of next 4 RS rows. Mark left front for 6 buttons.

RIGHT FRONT

Work as for left front, reversing shaping and making buttonholes 1 st from edge, as marked: K1, YO, K2tog, resume patt. On following row, P the YO.

SLEEVES

With A, CO 60 (64, 70, 76) sts. Beg inc 1 st at each edge every other row 4 times until there are 68 (72, 78, 84) sts. Shape cap: BO 4 (5, 6, 6) sts at beg of next 2 rows. Dec 1 st each edge every other row to cap depth of 4½ (5, 5½, 6)". BO all sts.

COLLAR

With A, CO 88 (90, 92, 94) sts. Work patt as for body, inc 1 st at each edge every 3 rows 4 times until there are 96 (98, 100, 102) sts. On row 15, dec 1 st at each edge every 3 rows. When 26 rows are complete, BO all sts.

FINISHING

Sew shoulder, side, and sleeve seams. Sew sleeves into armhole edge. With WS facing, use kitchener stitch to sew collar invisibly to neck between first bound-off sts of lapel (point A). Sew angle of collar from beg to widest point, to top edge of lapel, leaving approx 1½" of lapel open (between points B and C).

EDGING

With size E crochet hook and Quicksilver, work 1 round sc and 1 round rev sc around entire bottom, front, and neck edges, working 3 sts in each corner of bottom, lapel, and collar points on first row only. Work same for bottom edge of sleeve. Sew buttons to left front.

Barry's Version

MATERIALS

Trendsetter Yarns

(A) 3 (4, 4, 4) balls Balboa (50g/150yds), color #16
(B) 4 (5, 6, 7) balls Flora (20g/72yds), color #202
(C) 3 (4, 4, 5) balls Sunshine (50g/95yds), color #53
1 pair of size 7 US needles, or size to obtain correct gauge
Size E crochet hook
6 small self-made buttons (see page 70)

GAUGE

20 sts and 34 rows = 4" in half linen stitch on size 7 needles

DIRECTIONS

Work as for Laura's Version, using yarn substitutions above. Use yarn C for all crocheted edgings.

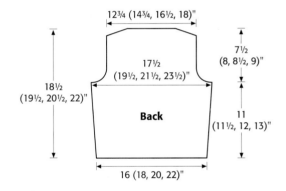

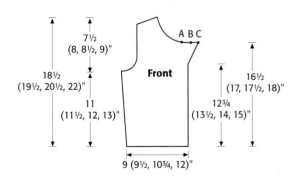

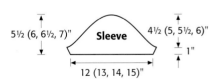

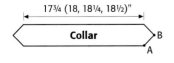

GRID LOCK

Designed by Barry Klein

BARRY'S VERSION (OPPOSITE): Dolcino was the perfect choice for this design because there is a large color range and every color combination we tried gave a different look to the design. It was important to me to play with color, and we made many different swatches to get the best effect. The lines created by changing direction and order are what make the design so special.

LAURA'S VERSION (ABOVE): The simple but bold stripes did indeed make the color choice of highest importance. I chose a textured cotton for contrast and added the interest of a cotton bouclé dyed in a multicolor that repeats the solids. I also turned the jacket into a pullover and shortened the sleeves a bit to show how simple changes can make a difference.

Barry's Version

Sizes

Small (Medium, Large, X-Large, XX-Large)

Knitted Measurements

(approx.)

Bust: 35 (38, 41, 44, 47)"

Materials

Trendsetter Yarns

(A) 5 (5, 6, 7, 8) balls Dolcino (50g/100yds), color #60

(B) 1 (2, 2, 2, 3) balls Dolcino, color #61

(C) 1 (2, 2, 2, 3) balls Dolcino, color #113

(D) 1 (2, 2, 2, 3) balls Dolcino, color #112

1 pair each of size 10 US and size 10½ US needles, or size to obtain correct gauge

Size G crochet hook

5 self-made buttons

SELF-MADE BUTTONS

With size G crochet hook and A, work sc around a 1"-diameter plastic ring to cover it; fasten off yarn, leaving a long tail. Thread long tail on a tapestry needle and run through the solid base of the sc sts on the inside of the ring. Pull the thread tightly. This will gather the sts toward the center and fill in the open space.

Gauge

17 sts and 24 rows = 4" in stock st on size 10½ needles

Note: *The back is worked in 2 pieces and sewn together.*

Right Back

With size 10 needles and A, CO 36 (40, 44, 47, 50) sts. Work in garter st for 3 rows. Change to size 10½ needle and work in stock st for 2 (2½, 2½, 3, 3)". Change to B, then C, then D, each for 2 (2½, 2½, 3, 3)". Change to A. At the same time, when 11½ (12½, 13½, 14, 14)" from CO or desired length to underarm, BO 5 (5, 6, 6, 7) sts at armhole edge once. Dec 1 st at armhole edge, using full-fashion dec (we used 2 edge sts), every other row 4 (5, 5, 6, 6) times until 27 (30, 33, 35, 37) sts remain. Cont until armhole is 6½ (7, 7½, 8, 8½)". BO 12 sts at neck edge once. Dec 1 st at neck edge every row 2 times. When armhole is 7 (7½, 8, 8½, 9)", BO rem sts.

Right Front

Work as for back until armhole is 4½ (5, 5½, 6, 6½)". BO 6 sts at neck edge once. BO 2 sts at neck edge once. Dec 1 st at neck edge every other row 6 times. Cont until same length as back. BO rem sts.

LEFT BACK

With size 10 needles and A, CO 36 (40, 44, 47, 50) sts. Work in garter st for 3 rows. Change to 10½ needle and stock st until 8 (10, 10, 12, 12)" from CO. Work as follows from armhole edge to neck edge: 9 (10, 11, 11, 12) sts with A; 9 (10, 11, 12, 12) sts with B; 9 (10, 11, 12, 13) sts with C; and 9 (10, 11, 12, 13) sts with D. Cont in vertical stripes in stock st, twisting yarn to avoid holes when changing color, until 11½ (12½, 13½, 14, 14)" from CO. BO 5 (5, 6, 6, 7) sts at armhole edge once. Dec 1 st at armhole edge, using full-fashion dec, every other row 4 (5, 5, 6, 6) times until there are 27 (30, 33, 35, 37) sts. Cont until armhole is 6½ (7, 7½, 8, 8½)". BO 12 sts at neck edge once. Dec 1 in C st at neck edge, using full-fashion dec, every row 2 times. Cont to same length as right back. BO rem sts.

LEFT FRONT

Work as for left back until armhole is 4½ (5, 5½, 6, 6½)". BO 6 sts at neck edge once. BO 2 sts at neck edge once. Dec 1 st in C at neck edge, using full-fashion dec, every other row 6 times. Cont until same as back. BO rem sts.

RIGHT SLEEVE

With size 10 needles and A, CO 50 (52, 54, 54, 56) sts. Work in K1, P1 rib for 1", inc 11 (10, 10, 10, 10) sts evenly across last row until there are 61 (62, 64, 64, 66) sts. Change to size 10½ needles and beg stock st, inc 1 st at each end every 9 (7, 9, 6, 7) rows 4 (5, 4, 6, 5) times until there are 69 (72, 72, 76, 76) sts. At the same time, when 3½ (4½, 3½, 5, 5)" from CO, work as follows: 2 (2½, 2½, 3, 3)" each of B, C, D, and A in that order. At the same time, when sleeve is 7" from CO, BO 5 (5, 6, 6, 7) sts at beg of next 2 rows. Dec 1 st at each end every other row 4 (5, 12, 12, 15) times, then every row 20 (20, 12, 14, 10) times. BO 2 sts at beg of next 2 rows. BO rem sts.

LEFT SLEEVE

With size 10 needles, CO 50 (52, 54, 54, 56) sts as follows: 0 (1, 0, 0, 0) with C; 6 (8, 9, 7, 6) with D; 8 (8, 9, 10, 11) with A; 7 (9, 9, 10, 11) with B; 8 (8, 9, 10, 11) with C; 7 (8, 9, 10, 11) with D; 8 (9, 9, 7, 6) with

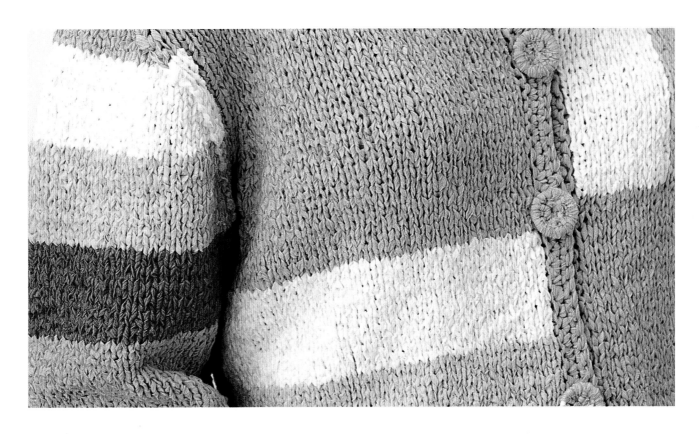

A; and 6 (1, 0, 0, 0) with B. Work in K1, P1 rib for 1", inc 0 (0, 0, 0, 0) sts with C; 2 (2, 1, 1, 1) with D; 1 (2, 2, 2, 2) with A; 2 (1, 2, 2, 2) with B; 1 (2, 2, 2, 2) with C; 2 (2, 2, 2, 2) with D; 1 (1, 1, 1, 1); and 2 (0, 0, 0, 0) with B across row until there are 61 (62, 64, 64, 66) sts. Change to size 10½ needles and beg stock st, inc 1 st at each end every 9 (7, 9, 6, 7) rows 4 (5, 4, 6, 5) times until there are 69 (72, 72, 76, 76) sts. At the same time, when sleeve is 3½ (4½, 3½, 5, 5)" from CO, change to A only and cont until sleeve is 7" from CO. BO 5 (5, 6, 6, 7) sts at beg of next 2 rows. Dec 1 st at each end every other row 4 (5, 12, 12, 15) times, then every row 20 (20, 12, 14, 10) times. BO 2 sts at beg of next 2 rows. BO rem sts.

FINISHING

Sew shoulder seams. Set sleeves to body. Sew center back, sleeve, and side seams. With size 10 needles and A, pick up 76 (78, 78, 80, 80) sts around neck edge. Work in K1, P1 rib for 2". BO in patt. With size G crochet hook and A, work 1 row of sc along right front edge. Work second row, making first button-hole 1" from neck edge and then every 3" to bottom. Work 1 row more of sc; fasten off. Rep the 3 rows of crochet on left front without buttonholes. Sew buttons to left front.

Laura's Version

MATERIALS

Prism Yarns

(A) 5 (6, 7, 8, 9) skeins Cotton Crepe (2oz/75yds), color #310 Sage

(B) 1 (2, 2, 3, 3) skeins Cotton Crepe, color #404 Blue

(C) 1 (2, 2, 3, 3) skeins Ruffles (2oz/85yds), color Mirage

(D) 1 (2, 2, 3, 3) skeins Cotton Crepe, color #503 Coral

1 pair of size 6 US needles, or size to obtain correct gauge

Size G crochet hook

GAUGE

17 sts and 24 rows = 4" in stock st on size 6 needles

BACK AND FRONT

Work as for Barry's Version, using yarn substitutions above.

RIGHT SLEEVE

Work as for original pattern, shortening sleeve by 2" by working to only 2 (2½, 3, 3, 3)" on first color. Finish sleeve as written, but beg cap shaping at 5" from CO. Cap will be same depth.

LEFT SLEEVE

Work as for original, shortening sleeve 2" by working stripes for full length, then beg cap shaping at 5" from CO.

FINISHING

Sew center front and back seams. Sew shoulder seams. Sew side and sleeve seams. Sew sleeves into armhole edge. With Color A and size G crochet hook, work 1 round sc around neck edge. With Color B, work 1 round rev sc around neck edge.

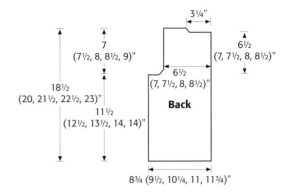

3¼"

7
(7½, 8, 8½, 9)"

6½
(7, 7½, 8, 8½)"

18½
(20, 21½, 22½, 23)"

6½
(7, 7½, 8, 8½)"

Back

11½
(12½, 13½, 14, 14)"

8¾ (9½, 10¼, 11, 11¾)"

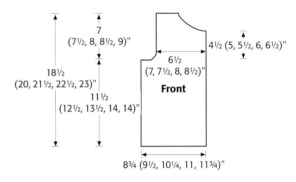

7
(7½, 8, 8½, 9)"

4½ (5, 5½, 6, 6½)"

18½
(20, 21½, 22½, 23)"

6½
(7, 7½, 8, 8½)"

Front

11½
(12½, 13½, 14, 14)"

8¾ (9½, 10¼, 11, 11¾)"

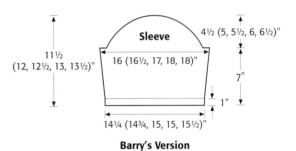

11½
(12, 12½, 13, 13½)"

Sleeve

16 (16½, 17, 18, 18)"

4½ (5, 5½, 6, 6½)"

7"

1"

14¼ (14¾, 15, 15, 15½)"

Barry's Version

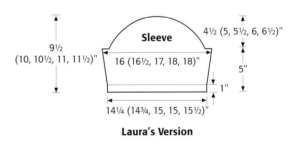

9½
(10, 10½, 11, 11½)"

Sleeve

16 (16½, 17, 18, 18)"

4½ (5, 5½, 6, 6½)"

5"

1"

14¼ (14¾, 15, 15, 15½)"

Laura's Version

QUILTED DELIGHT

Designed by Laura Bryant

LAURA'S VERSION (OPPOSITE): I have used this stitch before and love it. The yarns that I chose, Cleo and Trillino, are too limp and loose when knit on their own, but the slipping and quilting condenses them into a great hand. The electric colors suggested a modern silhouette, so I made the jacket somewhat cropped and slightly boxy with a narrow sleeve, and finished it with side vents and great glass buttons.

BARRY'S VERSION (ABOVE): I really liked the contrast of colors in Laura's original design and I wanted to keep that when selecting my yarns. I picked two favorites and made the first swatch using Charm, a novelty component yarn, as the inside yarn and Dolcino, a woven ribbon, as the outside. The pattern stitch got lost and the feel was hard. Reversing the two and shifting how the stitch was twisted, I was able to match Laura's stitch gauge and end up with a look I liked. A simple change was made from cardigan to pullover by working the front as one, and off I went.

Laura's Version

Sizes

Small (Medium, Large, X-Large)

Knitted Measurements

(approx.)
Bust (after blocking): 35 (40, 44, 48)"

Materials

Prism Yarns

(A) 6 (7, 8, 10) skeins Trillino (2oz/85yds), color #360

(B) 6 (7, 8, 10) skeins Cleo (1.5oz/82yds), color Cantina

1 pair of size 7 US needles, or size to obtain correct gauge

Size F crochet hook

4 medium glass buttons

Gauge

20 sts = 4.5"; 28 rows = 4" in quilted stitch (blocked)

Quilted Stitch

(multiple of 6 plus 2)

Row 1 (WS): With A, P1, *sl 3 wyib, P3*; rep from * to *, end P1.

Row 2: With B, *K5, sl 1 wyif*; rep from * to *, end K2.

Row 3: With B, P2, *sl 1 wyib, P5*; rep from * to *.

Row 4: With A, *K5, insert right-hand needle down behind loose color A strand of row 1; lift this strand over point of left-hand needle and K2tog-b (i.e., the color A strand and color A st that is on needle)*; rep from * to *, end K2.

Row 5: With A, P4, *sl 3 wyib, P3*; rep from * to *, end sl 3 wyib, P1.

Row 6: With B, K2, *sl 1 wyif, K5*; rep from * to *.

Row 7: With B, *P5, sl 1 wyib*; rep from * to *, end P2.

Row 8: With A, K2 *insert left-hand needle under color A strand of row 5, and K2tog-b as in row 4, K5*; rep from * to *.

Back

With color A, CO 80 (92, 98, 104) sts. Beg patt st and work to 11 (12, 13, 14)" from CO or desired length to underarm. BO 6 sts at beg of next 2 rows. BO 2 sts at beg of next 2 rows. Dec 1 st at each edge every other row 2 times, then every 4 rows 2 times until 56 (68, 74, 80) sts remain. When piece is 19 (20½, 22, 23)" from CO, ending with row 4 or 8, BO all sts firmly.

Front

With color A, CO 38 (44, 50, 56) sts. Work as for back to armhole, then shape armhole on one side only and at the same time, when piece is 12 (13, 14, 15)" from CO, shape neck: dec 1 st at center front edge every other row 12 (12, 13, 14) times. When same length as back, BO all sts firmly. Rep for other side, reversing shaping.

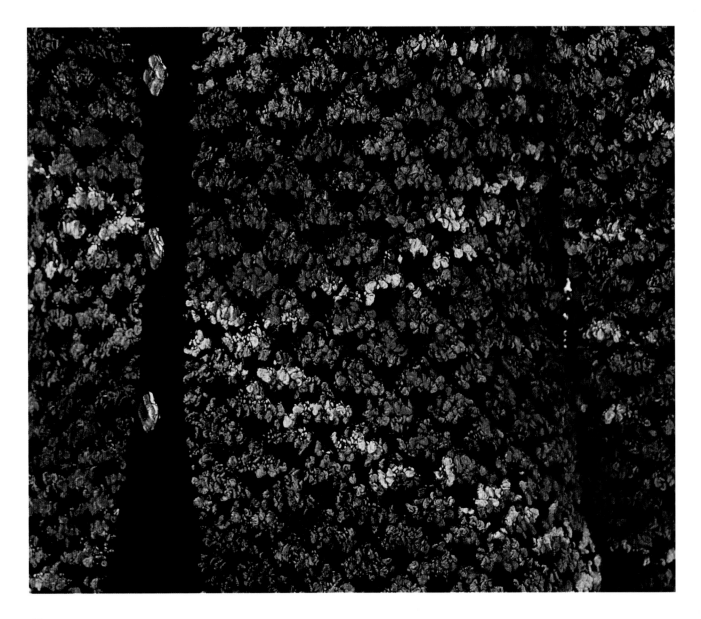

SLEEVES

With color A, CO 32 (32, 38, 38) sts. Work patt st, inc 1 st at each edge every 6 rows 12 (14, 13, 15) times, working new sts into patt as you are able until there are 56 (60, 64, 68) sts. When sleeve is 16 (16½, 17, 17½)" from CO or desired length, shape cap: BO 5 sts at beg of next 2 rows. Beg dec 1 st at each edge every other row until cap is 5 (5½, 6, 6)" deep. BO 5 sts at beg of next 2 rows. BO all rem sts.

FINISHING

Sew shoulder, sleeve, and side seams, leaving 3" open at bottom for side slits. Sew sleeves into armhole edges. With size F crochet hook and A, work 3 rows sc around entire front and neck edges. Work 3 sts at neck corners for first 2 rows, then work 2 sts at neck corners in rem rows. Measure left side for placement of 4 buttons, having bottom button at waist, then work 1 more row sc along front and neck edges, making button loops on RS to correspond to button placement. Work 1 round sc and 1 round rev sc around entire front, neck, and bottom edges, including side slits. Work 1 round sc and 1 round rev sc around each bottom edge of sleeve.

Barry's Version

MATERIALS

Trendsetter Yarns

(A) 11 (13, 15, 17) balls Charm (20g/90yds), color #310; worked 3 strands throughout

(B) 5 (6, 7, 8) balls Dolcino (50g/100yds), color #112

1 pair of size 10 US needles, or size to obtain correct gauge

Size F crochet hook

GAUGE

20 sts = 4.5"; 28 rows = 4" in modified quilted stitch (blocked)

MODIFIED QUILTED STITCH

Row 1 (WS): With A (tripled throughout), P1, ★ sl 3 wyif, P3★; rep from ★ to ★, end P1.

Row 2: With B, ★K5, sl 1 wyib★; rep from ★ to ★, end K2.

Row 3: With B, P2, ★sl 1 wyif, P5★; rep from ★ to ★.

Row 4: With A, ★K5, insert right needle down behind loose A strands of row 1. Lift strands over point of left needle and K2tog-b★; rep from ★ to ★, end K2.

Row 5: With A, P4, *sl 3 wyif, P3*; rep from * to *, end sl 3 wyif, P1.

Row 6: With B, K2, *sl 1 wyif, K5*; rep from * to *.

Row 7: With B, *P5, sl 1 wyib*; rep from * to *, end P2.

Row 8: With A, K2, *insert left needle under color A strands of row 5 from behind and K2tog-b as done in row 4, K5*; rep from * to *.

BACK

Work as for Laura's Version in modified quilted stitch on size 10 needles.

FRONT

Work as for back until 12½ (13, 13½, 14)" from CO. Divide work in half, joining new yarns and working both neck edges at same time. Cont in patt, dec 1 st each neck edge every other row 12 (12, 13, 14) times. Cont until same length as back. BO rem sts.

SLEEVES

Work as for Laura's Version in modified quilted stitch on size 10 needles.

FINISHING

Assemble as for Laura's Version. With size G crochet hook and B, work 2 rows of sc around neck edge. Work 1 row of rev sc around neck edge, alternating 1 st in B with 1 st in A (tripled). Fasten off. With size G crochet hook and B, work 1 row of sc along bottom edges of front, side vents, and back. Rep 1 row of sc along sleeve bottom.

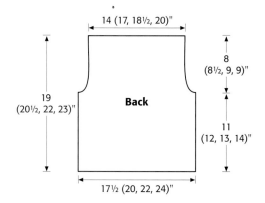

Back

14 (17, 18½, 20)"

19 (20½, 22, 23)"

8 (8½, 9, 9)"

11 (12, 13, 14)"

17½ (20, 22, 24)"

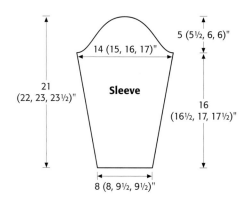

Sleeve

14 (15, 16, 17)"

5 (5½, 6, 6)"

21 (22, 23, 23½)"

16 (16½, 17, 17½)"

8 (8, 9½, 9½)"

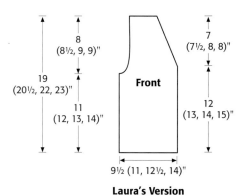

Front

8 (8½, 9, 9)"

7 (7½, 8, 8)"

19 (20½, 22, 23)"

11 (12, 13, 14)"

12 (13, 14, 15)"

9½ (11, 12½, 14)"

Laura's Version

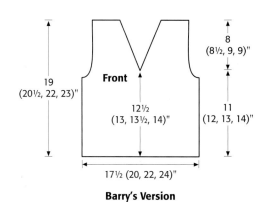

Front

8 (8½, 9, 9)"

19 (20½, 22, 23)"

12½ (13, 13½, 14)"

11 (12, 13, 14)"

17½ (20, 22, 24)"

Barry's Version

INTERLOCKING INTEREST

Designed by Barry Klein

BARRY'S VERSION (OPPOSITE): I just knew that I had to use Dune, a brushed kid mohair with a textured cotton/metallic component, for this design. The space-dyed colors are strong enough to stand on their own against the depth of Dolcino colors. The design was perfect for the color, texture, and a subtle ridge stitch that let the sparkle shine through.

LAURA'S VERSION (ABOVE): This is a beautiful set, one that could go "black tie." I chose hand-dyed sparkly Super Dazzle and Bon Bon ribbons in coordinating colors to sit underneath the texture. I expected the same gauge as Barry's version, but my swatch was smaller. Because the gauge was only half a stitch per inch different, I simply made the set one size larger to achieve the desired size; that is, I made a large to get a medium.

Barry's Version

SIZES

Small (Medium, Large, X-Large, XX-Large)

KNITTED MEASUREMENTS

(approx.)

Jacket Bust: 38 (42, 46, 50, 54)"

Shell Bust: 36 (40, 44, 48, 52)"

MATERIALS

Trendsetter Yarns

(A) 7 (8, 9, 10, 11) balls Dune (50g/90yds), color #76

(B) 2 (2, 3, 3, 4) balls Dolcino (50g/100yds), color #2

(C) 2 (3, 3, 3, 4) balls Dolcino, color #103

(D) 2 (3, 3, 3, 4) balls Dolcino, color #11

(E) 6 (7, 8, 8, 8) balls Dolcino, color #101

1 pair each of size 9 US and size 10 US needles, or size to obtain correct gauge

Size G crochet hook

GAUGES

22 sts x 25 rows = 5" in ridged stripe on size 10 needles

18 sts x 24 rows = 4" in stock st and E on size 10 needles

RIDGED STRIPE

Row 1 (RS): *K2 with A, K2 with B*; rep from * to *, end K2 with A.

Row 2: *P2 with A, P2 with B*; rep from * to *, end P2 with A.

Row 3: With B, knit across.

Row 4: With B, purl across.

Row 5: Rep row 1.

Row 6: Rep row 2.

Rows 7 and 8: With A, knit across.

Rep rows 1–8, alternating C, D, and E for B.

JACKET BACK

With size 9 needles and A, CO 86 (94, 102, 110, 118) sts. Work in garter st for 6 rows. Change to size 10 needles and knit back across row. Beg ridged stripe pattern and work until 13" from CO or desired length to underarm. BO 6 (7, 8, 9,10) sts at beg of next 2 rows. Dec 1 st at each end every other row 6 (7, 8, 9, 10) times until 62 (66, 70, 74, 78) sts remain. Cont until armhole is 8 (8½, 8½, 9, 9)". BO rem sts.

JACKET FRONTS

With size 9 needles and A, CO 38 (42, 46, 50, 54) sts. Work in garter st for 6 rows. Change to size 10 needles and knit back across row. Beg ridged stripe pattern and work until same length as back. BO 6 (7, 8, 9, 10) sts at armhole edge once. Dec 1 st at armhole edge every other row 6 (7, 8, 9, 10) times until 62 (66, 70, 74, 78) sts remain. Cont until armhole is 5½ (6, 6, 6½, 6½)". BO 5 sts at neck edge once. Dec 1 st at neck edge every row 8 times. Cont to same length as back. BO rem sts. Make second front, reversing shaping.

JACKET SLEEVES

With size 9 needles and A, CO 30 (30, 32, 32, 32) sts. Work in garter st for 10 rows, inc 20 (20, 18, 18, 18) sts evenly across last row. Change to size 10 needles and knit back across row. Beg ridged stripe pattern, inc 1 st at each end every 6 (5, 5, 5, 5) rows 12 (14, 14, 14, 14) times until there are 74 (78, 78, 78, 78) sts. Cont until sleeve is 17 (17, 17½, 17½, 17½)" from CO or desired length. BO 6 (7, 8, 9,10) sts at beg of next 2 rows. Dec 1 st at each end every other row 5 (6, 5, 10, 10) times, then at each end every row 20 (20, 20, 14, 14) times. BO 2 sts at beg of next 2 rows. BO rem sts.

JACKET FINISHING

Sew shoulder seams. Sew sleeves to body. Sew underarm and side seams. With size 9 needles and A, pick up 70 (72, 74, 76, 76) sts along front edge. Work in garter st for 5 rows. BO. Rep for other front. With size 9 needles and A, pick up 80 (82, 84, 86, 86) sts around neck edge. Work in garter st for 8 rows. BO. With size G crochet hook and E, work 1 row of sl st around front bands, neck edge, bottom edge, and sleeve cuffs.

SHELL BACK

With size 9 needles and A, CO 82 (90, 98, 106, 114) sts. Work in garter st for 6 rows. Change to size 10 needles and knit back across row. Beg ridged stripe pattern, working with C, D, and E in that order one time only. Cont with E in stock st until 11 (11½, 12, 12, 12½)" from CO or desired length to underarm. BO 6 (7, 8, 8, 9) sts at beg of next 2 rows. Dec 1 st at each end every other row 7 (8, 8, 9, 9) times until 56 (60, 66, 72, 78) sts remain. Cont until armhole is 6½ (6½, 7, 7½, 7½)". BO center 22 sts. Join new yarn and work both neck edges at same time. Dec 1 st at each neck edge every row 2 times. Cont until armhole is 7 (7, 7½, 8, 8)". BO rem sts.

SHELL FRONT

Work as for shell back until armhole is 5 (5, 5½, 6, 6)". BO center 12 sts. Join new yarn and work both neck edges at same time. BO 2 sts at each neck edge once. Dec 1 st at each neck edge, using full-fashion dec, every other row 5 times. Cont until same length as back. BO rem sts.

SHELL FINISHING

Sew shoulder seams. With size 10 needles and E, pick up 70 (72, 74, 74, 76) sts around neck edge. Work in garter st for 3 rows. BO. With size 10 needles and E, pick up 64 (68, 70, 72, 72) sts along armhole edge. Work in garter st for 3 rows. BO. Sew side seams.

Laura's Version

Sizes

Petite (Small, Medium, Large, X-Large)

Knitted Measurements

(approx.)
34 (38, 42, 46, 50)"

Materials

Prism Yarns

(A) 7 (8, 9, 10, 11) skeins Super Dazzle (1oz/90yds),
    color Embers

(B) 7 (8, 9, 10, 11) skeins Bon Bon (2oz/94yds),
    color #107

(C) 2 (2, 3, 3, 4) skeins Bon Bon, color #102

(D) 2 (2, 3, 3, 4) skeins Bon Bon, color #201

(E) 2 (2, 3, 3, 4) skeins Bon Bon, color #104

1 pair each of size 6 US and size 7 US needles, or size
    to obtain correct gauge

Gauges

25 sts and 30 rows = 5" in ridged stripe on size 7
    needles

20 sts and 28 rows = 4" in stock st and Bon Bon on
    size 7 needles

Directions

Work as for Barry's Version, using yarn substitutions above. Make one size larger than desired size to accommodate the difference in gauge. Use B for the body of the shell.

Jacket Bands

With size 6 needles and B, pick up and K 94 (96, 98, 100, 100) sts along front edge. K 3 more rows with B. K 2 rows with A. K 4 rows with B, then BO. Rep for other front. Beg at right front neck with B, pick up and K 23 (24, 25, 26, 27) sts to shoulder, 40 sts across back neck, and 23 (24, 25, 26, 27) sts to left front neck. K 3 rows with B. K 2 rows with A. K 4 rows with B. BO all sts.

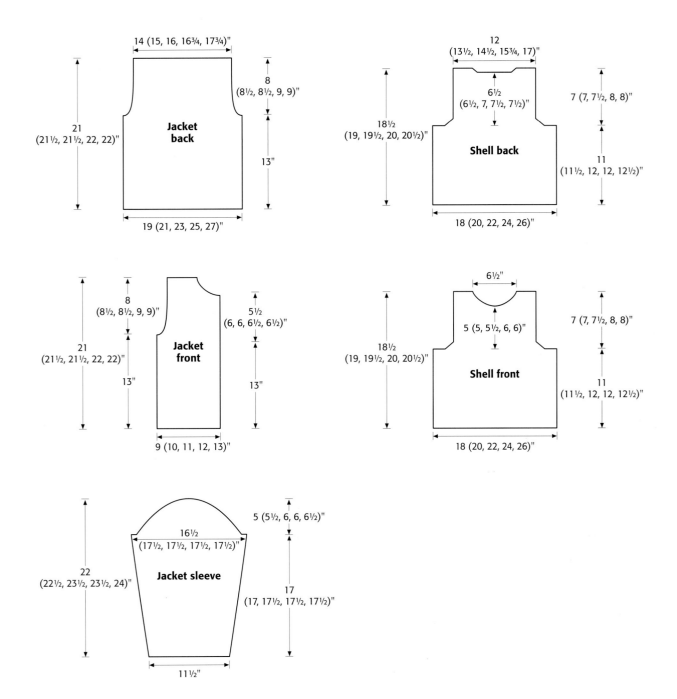

Jacket back

14 (15, 16, 16¾, 17¾)"

8 (8½, 8½, 9, 9)"

21 (21½, 21½, 22, 22)"

13"

19 (21, 23, 25, 27)"

Shell back

12 (13½, 14½, 15¾, 17)"

6½ (6½, 7, 7½, 7½)"

7 (7, 7½, 8, 8)"

18½ (19, 19½, 20, 20½)"

11 (11½, 12, 12, 12½)"

18 (20, 22, 24, 26)"

Jacket front

8 (8½, 8½, 9, 9)"

5½ (6, 6, 6½, 6½)"

21 (21½, 21½, 22, 22)"

13"

13"

9 (10, 11, 12, 13)"

Shell front

6½"

5 (5, 5½, 6, 6)"

7 (7, 7½, 8, 8)"

18½ (19, 19½, 20, 20½)"

11 (11½, 12, 12, 12½)"

18 (20, 22, 24, 26)"

Jacket sleeve

16½ (17½, 17½, 17½, 17½)"

5 (5½, 6, 6, 6½)"

22 (22½, 23½, 23½, 24)"

17 (17, 17½, 17½, 17½)"

11½"

TEXTURED TWOSOME

Designed by Laura Bryant

LAURA'S VERSION (OPPOSITE): I love the look of eyelash yarns, but find I often feel too big in an allover eyelash garment. Fern is a continuous eyelash yarn with a thickness that takes it from being a component yarn to one that can be knit on its own. I paired it with Diana, a tubular rayon ribbon whose gauge is similar. Rows of Fern are gradually added to a basic Diana body. Most of the lash appears in the shoulder area, giving a more slimming silhouette. A sand-washed solid shell trimmed in the jacket's multicolor yarn completes the set.

BARRY'S VERSION (ABOVE): One of the fun things to do when selecting yarns is to try opposite yarns. Since Laura used a flat yarn for the body with eyelashes as the detail, I thought it would work with Dancer, a short eyelash yarn wrapped around a French cut lace for the body, with the stripes in Dolcino, our flat woven ribbon. With an overall short lash look, the jacket remained slimming and kept Laura's original effect.

Laura's Version

Sizes

Small (Medium, Large, X-Large)

Knitted Measurements

(approx.)
Jacket Bust: 38 (42, 46, 50)"
Shell Bust: 36 (38, 42, 46)"

Materials

Prism Yarns

(MC) 11 (12, 14, 15) skeins Diana (2oz/55yds), color
     Tumbleweed

(CC) 3 (3, 3, 4) skeins Fern (2oz/45yds), color
     Tumbleweed

(A) 6 (7, 8, 10) skeins Diana, color #309

1 pair each of size 10 US and size 11 US needles, or
     size to obtain correct gauge

Stitch markers

4 large buttons

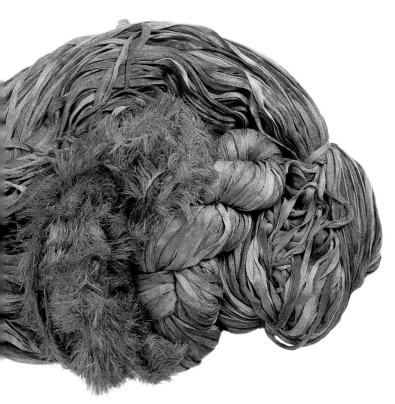

Gauge

12 sts and 20 rows = 4" in stock st and Diana on size
     11 needles

NOTE: *The stripe sequence is based on a naturally occurring sequence of numbers known as Fibonacci numbers. When you are working many rows of Diana after adding Fern, cut the latter after 2 rows and weave in; when you get near the top and there are fewer rows between, you can carry Fern loosely up the side.*

Pattern Repeat

16 rows stock st, MC

2 rows garter st, CC

10 rows stock st, MC

2 rows garter st, CC

6 rows stock st, MC

2 rows garter st, CC

4 rows stock st, MC

2 rows garter st, CC

2 rows stock st, MC

Jacket Back

With size 10 needles and MC, CO 58 (64, 70, 76) sts. Work 4 rows in garter st, then change to size 11 needles and work pattern repeat as noted above. When 12 (13, 14, 15)" from CO or desired length to underarm, BO 3 (4, 5, 5) sts at beg of next 2 rows. BO 2 sts at beg of next 2 rows. Dec 1 st at each edge every other row 4 times, then every 4 rows 0 (0, 1, 1) time until 44 (48, 50, 52) sts remain. Cont in pattern repeat as above to 20 (21, 22½, 24)" from CO, repeating last 4 rows as necessary. BO all sts firmly.

Jacket Fronts

With size 10 needles and MC, CO 29 (32, 35, 38) sts. Work as for back to armhole. Shape armhole on one side only and at the same time, beg shaping neck: dec 1 st at neck edge every 4 rows 8 (9, 9, 10) times until 14 (15, 16, 18) sts remain. When same length as back, BO all sts. Rep for other front, reversing shaping.

Jacket Sleeves

With size 10 needles and MC, CO 26 (28, 30, 32) sts. Work 4 rows garter st, then change to size 11 needles and work in pattern repeat, inc 4 sts, evenly spaced, across next row until there are 30 (32, 34, 36) sts. Inc 1 st at each edge every 6 rows 8 (8, 9, 10) times until there are 46 (48, 52, 56) sts. When sleeve is 15 (16, 16½, 17)" from CO or desired length, shape cap: BO 3 sts at beg of next 2 rows. Dec 1 st at each edge every other row 12 (12, 13, 14) times. BO 2 sts at beg of next 4 rows until 8 (10, 12, 14) sts remain. BO rem sts.

Jacket Finishing

Sew shoulder seams firmly. Sew side and sleeve seams. Sew sleeves into armhole edges.

Jacket Neckband

With size 10 needles and MC, pick up and K 44 (48, 52, 56) sts along right front to beg of neck shaping, place marker; pick up and K 32 (34, 36, 38) sts to shoulder; 20 (20, 22, 22) sts along back neck; 32 (34, 36, 38) sts to neck shaping; place marker; pick up and K 44 (48, 52, 56) sts to bottom. Work 10 rows garter st, inc 1 st on neck side of each front marker every other row and dec 1 st at each shoulder seam every 4 rows. At the same time, work 4 buttonholes in RS on row 5. BO. Sew buttons to left side.

Tip

Use a smaller needle when binding off. Since Diana is a fairly thick yarn, you need a tighter BO than you might think to make the front edge lie flat.

Shell Back

With size 10 needles and MC, CO 46 (50, 56, 62) sts. Work 4 rows garter st. Change to size 11 needles and A, beg stock st, inc 8 sts, evenly spaced, across first

row until there are 54 (58, 64, 70) sts. Work even to 10 (11, 12, 13)" from CO or desired length to underarm. BO 3 sts at beg of next 2 rows. BO 2 sts at beg of next 2 rows. Dec 1 st at each edge every other row 2 (2, 2, 3) times until 40 (44, 50, 54) sts remain. Work even to 17½ (19, 20½, 22)" from CO. BO all sts.

SHELL FRONT

Work as for back to 15 (16, 17, 18)", then shape neck: BO center 8 sts, then working each shoulder separately, BO at each neck edge 2 sts once. Dec 1 st at each edge every other row 2 (2, 3, 3) times until 12 (14, 16, 18) sts remain on each side. Work to same length as back, then BO all sts.

SHELL FINISHING

Sew one shoulder seam. With size 10 needles and MC, pick up and K 50 (50, 54, 54) sts along neck edge. Work 2 rows garter st, then BO evenly, making sure that edge lies flat but does not pull. Sew other shoulder seam. With size 10 needles and MC, pick up and K 52 (54, 56, 58) sts along armhole edge. Work 2 rows garter st, then BO all sts firmly. Rep for other armhole. Sew side seams.

Barry's Version

MATERIALS

Trendsetter Yarns

(MC) 7 (9, 11, 15) balls Dancer (50g/64yds), color #507

(A) 1 (1, 2, 2) balls Dolcino (50g/100yds), color #103

(B) 1 (1, 2, 2) balls Dolcino, color #8

(C) 4 (5, 6, 7) balls Dolcino, color #111

1 pair each of size 10 US and size 11 US needles, or size to obtain correct gauge

Stitch markers

4 large buttons

GAUGE

12 sts and 20 rows = 4" in stock st and MC on size 11 needles

BACK, FRONT, AND SLEEVES

Work as for Laura's Version, using yarn substitutions above and alternating A and B for CC every other stripe.

SWEATER FINISHING

Assemble as for Laura's Version. Work bands as original, alternating 2 rows A, 2 rows B in garter st for a total of 10 rows. BO.

Shell Back

With size 10 needles and A, CO as for Laura's instructions and knit back across row. Change to B and cont in garter st, alternating 2 rows A and 2 rows B for a total of 8 rows. Change to size 11 needles and C; work as for Laura's version.

Shell Front

Work as for back, following Laura's instructions for neck.

Shell Finishing

Sew 1 shoulder seam. With size 10 needles and A, pick up 44 (44, 48, 48) sts around neck edge and knit back across row. Change to B and knit 2 rows. BO. Sew other shoulder seam. With size 10 needles and A, pick up 52 (54, 56, 58) sts along armhole edge and knit back across row. Change to B and knit 2 rows. BO. Rep for other armhole. Sew side seams.

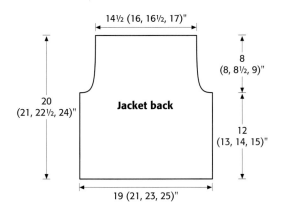

Jacket back

14½ (16, 16½, 17)"
8 (8, 8½, 9)"
20 (21, 22½, 24)"
12 (13, 14, 15)"
19 (21, 23, 25)"

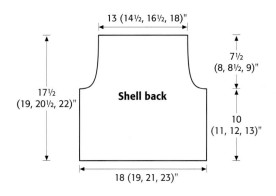

Shell back

13 (14½, 16½, 18)"
7½ (8, 8½, 9)"
17½ (19, 20½, 22)"
10 (11, 12, 13)"
18 (19, 21, 23)"

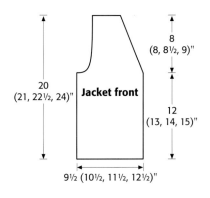

Jacket front

8 (8, 8½, 9)"
20 (21, 22½, 24)"
12 (13, 14, 15)"
9½ (10½, 11½, 12½)"

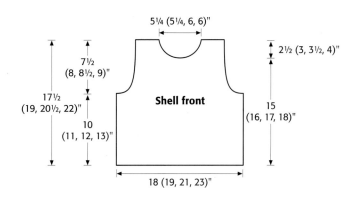

Shell front

5¼ (5¼, 6, 6)"
2½ (3, 3½, 4)"
7½ (8, 8½, 9)"
17½ (19, 20½, 22)"
10 (11, 12, 13)"
15 (16, 17, 18)"
18 (19, 21, 23)"

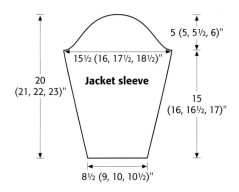

Jacket sleeve

5 (5, 5½, 6)"
15½ (16, 17½, 18½)"
20 (21, 22, 23)"
15 (16, 16½, 17)"
8½ (9, 10, 10½)"

ULTIMATE ELEGANCE

Designed by Barry Klein

BARRY'S VERSION (OPPOSITE): With this slip-stitch pattern, I wanted the texture to be used as detail. Luminato became the perfect companion yarn to Dolcino; the sparkling texture plays its part as it seems to weave in and out. The contrast between flat and novelty complements the stitch pattern.

LAURA'S VERSION (ABOVE): Dolcino is a yarn I have loved for years and is a great base on which to build textured yarns. I decided to keep the Dolcino and exchange only the accent yarn. A switch to rich teal colors allows the Peacock Wild Stuff to fade in and out in importance, adding a playful character to the set.

Barry's Version

SIZES

Small (Medium, Large, X-Large)

KNITTED MEASUREMENTS

(approx.)
Jacket Bust: 38 (42, 46, 50)"
Shell Bust: 36 (40, 44, 48)"

MATERIALS

Trendsetter Yarns

(MC) 16 (17, 18, 19) balls Dolcino (50g/100yds), color #5

(CC) 4 (5, 6, 7) balls Luminato (50g/82yds), color #742

1 pair each of size 9 US and size 10 US needles, or size to obtain correct gauge

Size G crochet hook

Stitch holders

3 round, cut-marble, ball buttons (Trendsetter buttons #69333B)

GAUGES

17 sts and 27 rows = 4" in sl st on size 10 needles
18 sts and 24 rows = 4" in stock st and MC on size 10 needles

SLIP STITCH

Rows 1, 3, 7, 11, 13, 17: With MC, knit across.

Rows 2, 4, 8, 12, 14, 18: With MC, purl across.

Rows 5 and 9: With CC, K1, sl 1 wyib, *K5, sl 3 wyib*; rep from * to *, end K5, sl 2 wyib, K1.

Rows 6 and 10: With CC, K1, sl 2 wyif, *K5, sl 3 wyif*; rep from * to *, end K5, sl 1 wyif, K1.

Rows 15 and 19: With CC, K3, *sl 3 wyib, K5*; rep from * to *, end sl 3 wyib, K4.

Rows 16 and 20: With CC, K4, *sl 3 wyif, K5*; rep from * to *, end sl 3 wyif, K3.

JACKET BACK

With size 9 needles and MC, CO 82 (86, 90, 94) sts. Work in K2, P2 rib for 2", inc 0 (4, 8, 12) sts evenly across last row until there are 82 (90, 98, 106) sts. Change to size 10 needles and work sl st patt until 13 (14, 14, 14)" from CO or desired length to under-arm. BO 5 (6, 7, 8) sts at beg of next 2 rows. Dec 1 st at each end every other row 6 (7, 8, 9) times until 60 (64, 68, 72) sts remain. Cont until armhole is 7½ (8, 8½, 9)". BO all sts.

JACKET FRONTS

NOTE: *Work both fronts at same time, working from left front to right front across RS row.*

With size 9 needles and MC, CO 42 (46, 48, 50) sts for each front. Work in K2, P2 rib for 1", ending ready for a RS row. Work across, making a button-hole on sts 3 and 4 at center edge of right front. Cont in rib for 1" more; end with a WS row, inc 1 (1, 3, 5) sts evenly across row. Change to size 10 needles and work as follows: 38 (42, 46, 50) sts in sl st patt. Place rem 5 sts at center edge of left front onto stitch holder. Slip first 5 sts from right front to stitch holder. Join yarn and work rem 38 (42, 46, 50) sts in sl st patt. Cont patt from left front (for small and large, the patt will break in the middle of a rep; cont rep across to right front, as if there were no break). Work to 12" from CO. Cont in patt, dec 1 st at each center edge every 4 (5, 5, 5) rows 13 times. At the same time, when 13 (14, 14, 14)" from CO or desired length to underarm, BO 5 (6, 7, 8) sts at armhole edge once. Dec 1 st at each armhole edge every other row 6 (7, 8, 9) times. Cont to same length as back. BO rem sts.

JACKET SLEEVES

With size 9 needles and MC, CO 34 (34, 38, 38) sts. Work in K2, P2 rib for 2", inc 16 (16, 12, 12) sts evenly across last row. Change to size 10 needles and work sl st patt on 50 sts, inc 1 st at each end every 9 rows 11 times and work new sts into patt whenever possible until there are 72 sts. Cont until sleeve is 17 (17, 17½, 17½)" from CO or desired length. BO 5 (6, 7, 8) sts at beg of next 2 rows. Dec 1 st at each end of every other row 14 (18, 22, 21) times, then 1 st at each end of every row 10 (5, 0, 0) times. BO 2 sts at beg of next 2 rows. BO rem sts.

JACKET FINISHING

Sew shoulder seams tightly. Sew sleeves to body by centering cap to shoulder seam. Sew underarm and side seams. With size 9 needles and MC, pick up sts from right front stitch holder. Cont in K2, P2 rib, making a buttonhole at 1½" from pickup and every 2½" up to neck shaping. Cont in rib st to center back neck. BO in patt. Weave band in place. With size 9 needles and MC, pick up sts from left front holder. Work in rib st to center back neck. BO. Weave band to front and join center back neck. Sew buttons to left front.

SHELL BACK

With size 9 needles and MC, CO 76 (84, 92, 100) sts. Work in K2, P2 rib for 1". Change to size 10 needles and stock st, inc 1 st at each end every 12 rows 3 times until there are 82 (90, 98, 106) sts. Cont until 11 (11, 11½, 12)" from CO or desired length to underarm. BO 6 (7, 7, 8) sts at beg of next 2 rows. Dec 1 st at each end, using full-fashion dec, every other row 6 (7, 8, 8) times. Cont until armhole is 6½ (7, 7, 7½)". BO center 22 sts. Join new yarn and work both neck edges at same time. Dec 1 st at each neck edge every row 3 times. Cont until armhole is 7 (7½, 7½, 8)". BO rem sts.

SHELL FRONT

Work as for back until armhole is 4½ (5, 5, 5½)". BO center 12 sts. Join new yarn and work both neck edges at same time. BO 2 sts at each neck edge once. Dec 1 st at each neck edge every other row 6 times. Cont to same length as back. BO rem sts.

SHELL FINISHING

Sew left shoulder seam. With size 9 needles and MC, pick up 82 (82, 82, 82) sts around neck edge. Start with row 2 of sl st patt and work 1 complete rep. BO. Sew right shoulder. Sew side seam. With size G crochet hook and MC, work 1 round of sc and 1 round of rev sc around armhole edge.

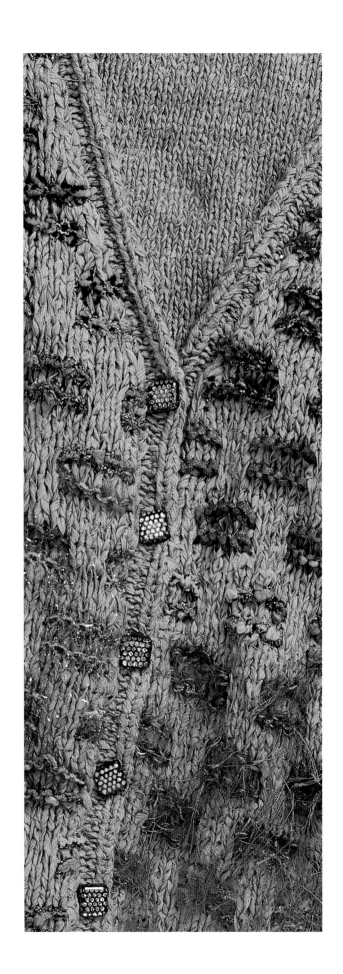

Laura's Version

MATERIALS

(MC) 16 (17, 18, 19) skeins Trendsetter Dolcino (50g/100yds), color #106

(CC) 1 (1½, 1½, 2) skeins Prism Wild Stuff (6–8oz/400yds), color Peacock

1 pair each of size 9 US and size 10 US needles, or size to obtain correct gauge

Size G crochet hook

Stitch holders

6 Dichroic glass buttons, 1" square

GAUGES

17 sts and 27 rows = 4" in sl st on size 10 needles

18 sts and 24 rows = 4" in stock st and MC on size 10 needles

DIRECTIONS

Work as for Barry's Version, using yarn substitutions above. Add 1 round sc and 1 round rev sc to neck edge of shell.

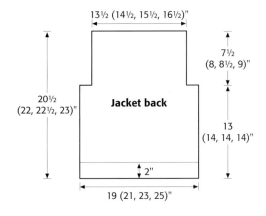

13½ (14½, 15½, 16½)"

7½ (8, 8½, 9)"

20½ (22, 22½, 23)"

Jacket back

13 (14, 14, 14)"

2"

19 (21, 23, 25)"

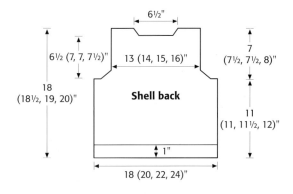

6½"

6½ (7, 7, 7½)"

13 (14, 15, 16)"

7 (7½, 7½, 8)"

18 (18½, 19, 20)"

Shell back

11 (11, 11½, 12)"

1"

18 (20, 22, 24)"

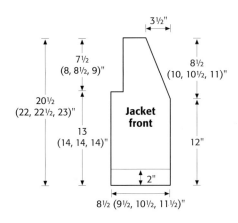

3½"

7½ (8, 8½, 9)"

8½ (10, 10½, 11)"

20½ (22, 22½, 23)"

Jacket front

13 (14, 14, 14)"

12"

2"

8½ (9½, 10½, 11½)"

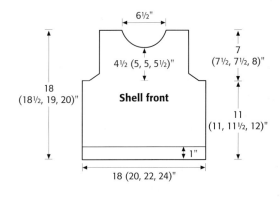

6½"

4½ (5, 5, 5½)"

7 (7½, 7½, 8)"

18 (18½, 19, 20)"

Shell front

11 (11, 11½, 12)"

1"

18 (20, 22, 24)"

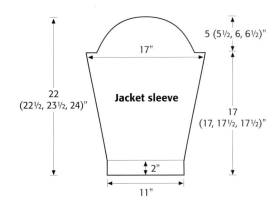

5 (5½, 6, 6½)"

17"

22 (22½, 23½, 24)"

Jacket sleeve

17 (17, 17½, 17½)"

2"

11"

PINSTIPES AND PUCKERS

Designed by Laura Bryant

LAURA'S VERSION (OPPOSITE): The mosaic stitch used in this sweater has long fascinated me. The lines of pinstriping pull the fabric up, allowing long stretches of stockinette to drape between them. The yarn I chose, Soft, is indeed soft enough to drape, and it is almost too soft and limp when knit alone. The pinstriping firms it up enough to give structure to the body, and the pinstriped sleeves and collar add a tailored touch.

BARRY'S VERSION (ABOVE): I wanted to have a contrast of solid and flat against textured and multicolored, so I selected Balboa and Dune. In swatching, I found that only by changing the stockinette to garter was I able to match gauge and maintain the look. The firmness of the pinstriping at the center made it easy to change the pullover into a cardigan by extending the center pinstripe on each separate front to a full section instead of splitting it in half.

Laura's Version

Sizes

Small (Medium, Large, X-Large)

Knitted Measurements

(approx.)

Bust: 41 (46, 50¾, 54½)"

Materials

Prism Yarns

(A) 6 (7, 9, 10) skeins Soft (1.5oz/88yds),
    color Smoke

(B) 6 (7, 8, 10) skeins Soft, color Fog

1 pair of size 8 US needles, or size to obtain correct
    gauge

Stitch markers

NOTE: *Because the pattern is a large repeat, sizing is accomplished by adjusting the number of stitches in each repeat. A gauge is given for each size, and the pattern repeat is bracketed for each size. The sizes have the same number of repeats, 4, which centers a strip of pinstriping.*

Gauge

In puckered st, S: 30 sts = 7.25"; M: 32 sts = 7.75"; L: 34 sts = 8.25"; XL: 40 sts — 9.25". All sizes, 28 rows = 4" in slipped areas

In pinstripe st, 19 sts and 28 rows = 4"

Puckered Mosaic Stitch

Multiple of 19 (21, 23, 25) sts plus 11 (11, 11, 13)

Row 1: With B, (K1, sl 1 wyib) 5 (5, 5, 6) times, *K10 (12, 14, 14), sl 1 wyib, (K1, sl 1 wyib) 4 (4, 4, 5) times*; rep from * to *, end K1.

Row 2: With B, (P1, sl 1 wyif) 5 (5, 5, 6) times, *P10 (12, 14, 14), sl 1 wyif, (P1, sl 1 wyif) 4 (4, 4, 5) times*; rep from * to *, end P1.

Row 3: With A, K2, sl 1 wyib, (K1, sl 1 wyib) 3 (3, 3, 4) times; *K12 (14, 16, 16), sl 1 wyib, (K1, sl 1 wyib) 3 (3, 3, 4) times*; rep from * to *, end K2.

Row 4: With A, P2, sl 1 wyif, (P1, sl 1 wyif) 3 (3, 3, 4) times, *P12 (14, 16, 16), sl 1 wyif, (P1, sl 1 wyif) 3 (3, 3, 4) times*; rep from * to *, end P2.

Rep rows 1–4.

Pinstripe for Sleeves and Collar Only

(worked on odd number of sts)

Row 1: With B, *K1, sl 1 wyib*; rep from * to *, end K1.

Row 2: With B, *P1, sl 1 wyif*; rep from * to *, end P1.

Row 3: With A, K1, *K1, sl 1 wyib*; rep from * to *, end K2.

Row 4: With A, P1, *P1, sl 1 wyif*; rep from * to *, end P2.

Rep rows 1–4.

BACK

With A, CO 87 (95, 103, 113) sts. Work puckered mosaic st to 11½, (12, 13, 14½)" from CO or desired length to underarm. BO 19 (21, 23, 25) sts at beg of next 2 rows until 47 (53, 59, 63) sts remain. Cont in patt st to 20 (21, 23, 25)" from CO. BO all sts firmly.

FRONT

Work as for back until armhole is 6 (6½, 7½, 8½)", then shape neck: BO center 7 (9, 9, 11) sts. Join yarn to RS and work both sides at same time; BO 3 sts at each neck edge once, BO 2 sts once. Dec 1 st at each neck edge every other row once until 14 (16, 19, 20) sts remain. When same length as back, BO all sts firmly.

SLEEVES

With A, CO 41 (43, 45, 47) sts. In pinstripe pattern, work 6 sts, place marker, work 1 st, place marker; work 28 (30, 32, 34) sts, place marker, work 1 st, place marker; work to end. Beg inc 1 st in the first st between pairs of markers, every 6 rows 18 times, working new sts into patt until there are 77 (79, 81, 83) sts. (This means that you will have 2 sts of the same color next to one another every other time you do an inc.) Keep to patt alignment as established, and allow those 2 sts to be the same. Isolating incs between markers keeps track of incs. After 18 incs have been made, on next sixth row, inc at beg and end of row to maintain pinstripe pattern. When sleeve is 19½, (20, 20½, 21)" from CO or desired length, shape cap: BO 4 sts at beg of next 18 (18, 18, 20) rows. BO rem sts loosely.

FINISHING

Sew left shoulder seam.

COLLAR

With A, pick up and K 28 (30, 32, 34) sts along back neck and 71 (73, 75, 77) sts around front neck until there are 99 (103, 107, 111) sts on needle. Work pinstripe pattern for 6 (7, 7, 8)", then BO all sts loosely.

FINISHING

Sew rem shoulder seam. Turn collar to inside and tack loosely along neckline. Sew sleeves into armhole edge, between bound-off sts. Sew side and sleeve seams, tacking edge of sleeve to bound-off armhole sts.

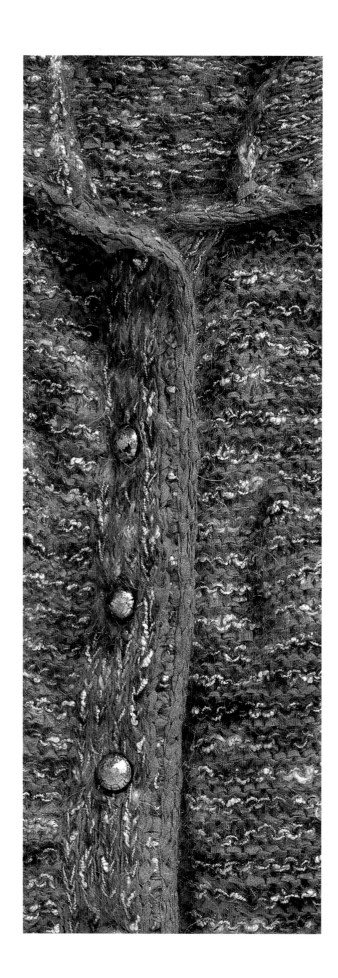

Barry's Version

MATERIALS

Trendsetter Yarns

(A) 5 (6, 7, 8) balls Balboa (50g/150yds), color #11

(B) 6 (7, 8, 9) balls Dune (50g/90yds), color #82

1 pair each of size 10 US and size 10½ US needles, or size to obtain correct gauge

Size G crochet hook

6 medium glass buttons (Trendsetter button #9341/24, color 2)

GAUGE

In modified pucker st, S: 30 sts = 7.25"; M: 32 sts = 7.75"; L: 34 sts = 8.25"; XL: 40 sts = 9.25" on size 10½ needles. All sizes, 32 rows = 4"

In pinstripe st, 19 sts and 28 rows = 4" on size 10½ needles

MODIFIED PUCKER STITCH

Multiple of 19 (21, 23, 25) sts plus 11 (11, 11, 13)

Row 1: With B, (K1, sl 1) 5 (5, 5, 6) times, *K10 (12, 14, 14), sl 1, (K1, sl 1) 4 (4, 4, 5) times*; rep from * to *, end K1.

Row 2: With B, (P1, sl 1) 5 (5, 5, 6) times, *K10 (12, 14, 14), sl 1, (P1, sl 1) 4 (4, 4, 5) times*; rep from * to *, end P1.

Row 3: With A, K2, sl 1, (K1, sl 1) 3 (3, 3, 4) times; *K12 (14, 16, 16), sl 1, (K1, sl 1) 3 (3, 3, 4) times*; rep from * to *, end K2.

Row 4: With A, P2, sl 1, (P1, sl 1) 3 (3, 3, 4) times, *K12 (14, 16, 16) sl 1, (P1, sl 1) 3 (3, 3, 4) times*; rep from * to *, end P2.

Rep rows 1–4.

BACK

Work as for Laura's Version with modified pucker st on size 10½ needles.

LEFT FRONT

With size 10½ needles and A, CO 49 (53, 57, 63) sts and knit back across row. Work in modified pucker st until 11½ (12, 13, 14½)" from CO or same length as back to underarm. BO 19 (21, 23, 25) sts at armhole edge once. Cont in patt until armhole is 6 (6½, 7½, 8½)"; BO 9 sts at neck edge once, BO 3 sts once, BO 2 sts once. Dec 1 st at neck edge once. Cont until front is same length as back. BO rem sts.

Mark left front for 6 buttons, beginning and ending 1" from top and bottom.

RIGHT FRONT

Work as for left front, reversing shaping. When 1" from CO, make one buttonhole in center of pinstripe band at center front edge. Rep buttonhole opposite marks on left front. Cont as for left front, reversing shaping. BO rem sts.

SLEEVES

Work as for Laura's Version on size 10½ needles.

FINISHING

Sew shoulder seams. With size 10 needles and A, pick up 103 (107, 110, 110) sts around neck edge, starting just inside of front pinstripe on right front and working around to same point on left front. Work in pinstripe pattern for 6". BO loosely. Fold collar to inside and tack in place at neck pickup row. Assemble as for Laura's Version. With size G crochet hook and A, work 1 row of sc and 1 row of sl st along the front and neck edges. Sew buttons to left front.

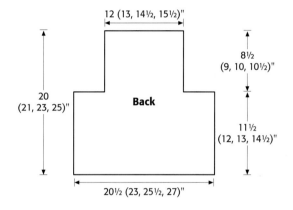

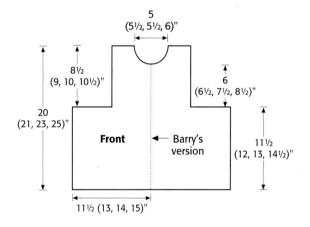

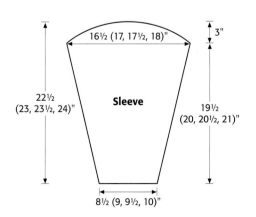

TEXTURE TWO WAYS

Designed by Barry Klein

BARRY'S VERSION (OPPOSITE): Savvy, a thick chenille wrapped with a short, black lash binder, was the yarn for this jacket because I wanted the body to be long and straight with crisp edges. To get this feel, we worked Savvy on a smaller needle. To keep the sleeves from being too thick, I used two different Merino style wools in a slip-stitch pattern that looks long and lean. These are easy yarns to work with in a quick knit that is timeless.

LAURA'S VERSION (ABOVE): This is a very wearable jacket that suggested a "blank canvas" to me. The body screams for the kind of texture Savvy created, so we used Impressions, another version of our "many yarns tied together" look. The neutral colors of the Prism Impressions, color Dune, were repeated in the sleeves, where one yarn is natural and one has been hand dyed. The use of a multicolor makes the pattern appear and disappear, adding a layer of mystery. I made ribbed cuffs on the sleeves because my yarns were not suited to a garter cuff.

Barry's Version

Sizes

Small (Medium, Large, X-Large)

Knitted Measurements

(approx.)
Bust: 38 (42, 46, 50)"

Materials

Trendsetter Yarns

(MC) 5 (6, 7, 8) hanks Savvy (100g/60yds), color #26

(A) 10 (10, 10, 10) balls Fashion Merino (50g/70yds), color #21

(B) 4 (5, 5, 5) balls Merino Kind (50g/137yds), color #735; worked in 2 strands throughout

1 pair each of size 11 US and size 13 US needles, or size to obtain correct gauge

Size H crochet hook

2 nickel-size buttons (Trendsetter buttons #61570)

Gauges

8 sts and 12 rows = 4" in stock st and Savvy on size 13 needles

15 sts and 24 rows = 4" in ribbed tweed st and A and B on size 11 needles

Ribbed Tweed Stitch

Row 1 (RS): With A, K3, *sl 1 wyib, K3*; rep from * to *.

Row 2: With A, K3, *sl 1 wyif, K3*; rep from * to *.

Row 3: With B, K1, *sl 1 wyib, K3*; rep from * to *, end sl 1 wyib, K1.

Row 4: With B, K1, *sl 1 wyif, K3*; rep from * to *, end sl 1 wyif, K1.

Rep rows 1–4.

Back

With size 13 needles and MC, CO 32 (36, 40, 44) sts. Work in stock st, inc 1 st at each end every other row 3 times until there are 38 (42, 46, 50) sts. Cont until 14 (15, 15, 16)" from CO or desired length to underarm. BO 2 (3, 3, 4) sts at beg of next 2 rows. Dec 1 st at each end every other row 3 (3, 4, 4) times until 28 (30, 32, 34) sts remain. Cont until armhole is 6½ (7½, 7½, 8)". BO center 10 sts. Join new yarn and work both neck edges at same time. Dec 1 st at each neck edge every row 2 times. Work 1 more row and BO rem sts.

Fronts

With size 13 needles and MC, CO 14 (16, 18, 20) sts. Work in stock st, inc 1 st at each end every other row 3 times until there are 20 (22, 24, 26) sts. Work until same length as back to underarm. BO 2 (3, 3, 4) sts at armhole edge once. Dec 1 st at armhole edge every other row 3 (3, 4, 4) times. Cont until armhole is 5 (6, 6, 6½)". BO 4 sts at neck edge once. Dec 1 st at neck edge every row 4 times. Cont until same length as back. BO rem sts.

SLEEVES

With size 13 needles and Savvy, CO 15 (16, 16, 17) sts. Work in garter st for 2½". Change to size 11 needle and A. Knit first RS row, inc 24 (23, 27, 30) sts evenly across row until there are 39 (39, 43, 47) sts and knit back across row. With B, beg ribbed tweed st on row 3. Work in patt, inc 1 st at each end every 9 rows 10 times and work new sts into patt when possible until there are 59 (59, 63, 67) sts. Cont in patt to 17 (17, 17, 17)" from CO or desired length, then shape cap: BO 4 (6, 6, 8) sts at beg of next 2 rows. Dec 1 st at each end every other row 10 (16, 18, 18) times. Dec 1 st at each end every row 10 (2, 2, 2) times. BO 2 sts at beg of next 2 rows. BO rem sts.

FINISHING

Sew shoulders. Sew sleeves to body. Sew sleeve and side seams, leaving body open at shaped edge. With size 11 needles and A, pick up and K 83 sts around neck edge and knit back across row. Beg ribbed tweed st on row 3 and work patt for 3" with B. BO in patt. With size H crochet hook and A, work 1 row of sc around fronts, making a loop buttonhole 1" down from neck shaping and 3" down from first buttonhole on right front. Cont around side vents, bottom edge, and neck. Work 1 more row of sl st to finish off. Sew buttons to left front.

Laura's Version

MATERIALS

Prism Yarns

(MC) 1½, (2, 2½, 3) skeins Impressions (6–8oz/150yds), color Dune

(A) 4 (4, 5, 5) skeins Grain (2oz/65yds), color Cream

(B) 3 (3, 4, 4) skeins Grain, color French Vanilla

1 pair of size 15 US needles for Impressions, or size to obtain correct gauge

1 pair each of size 9 US and size 11 US needles for sleeves, or size to obtain correct gauge

Size J crochet hook

6 textured shell buttons, 2" long (Trendsetter buttons #69627)

GAUGE

9 sts and 13 rows = 4" in stock st and Impressions on size 15 needles

15 sts and 24 rows = 4" in ribbed tweed st and A and B on size 11 needles

BACK

With size 15 needles and MC, CO 36 (40, 44, 48) sts. Work as for Barry's Version until armhole shaping. Cont armhole shaping, working 1 additional dec at each side edge after underarm shaping. Cont as for Barry's Version.

Fronts

With size 15 needles and MC, CO 18 (20, 22, 24) sts. Work as for Barry's Version until armhole shaping. Cont armhole shaping, working 1 additional dec at side edge after underarm shaping and 1 more st at neck edge. Cont as for Barry's Version.

Sleeves

With size 9 needles and A, CO 23 (25, 27, 29) sts. Work K1, P1 rib for 3", then change to size 11 needles and knit the first RS row, inc 16 (14, 16, 18) sts, evenly spaced, across row until there are 39 (39, 43, 47) sts. Work as for Barry's Version.

Finishing

Assemble as for Barry's Version. Front and bottom edges: With size J crochet hook and A, work 2 rounds sc around entire front, neck, and bottom edges, working 6 button loops, evenly spaced, along right front, 3 sts at neck corners, and 3 extra sts around each rounded edge of bottom, skipping the corner sts in side vents. Work 1 round rev sc around, working 1 st in each st and over chain button loop, and skipping 2 sts at vent. Sew buttons to left front.

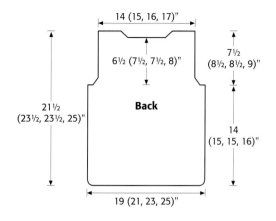

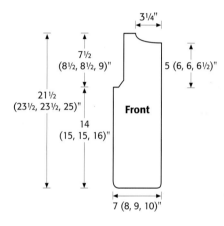

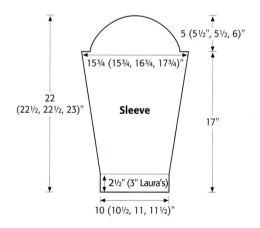

ALL TRIMMED UP

Designed by Laura Bryant

LAURA'S VERSION (OPPOSITE): Prism's Mohair, paired with light nylon Air, makes a great weight for a jacket. The body becomes a background for Light Stuff, an array of novelty yarns tied together. The yarns are all color-coordinated and gauge-coordinated, and alternate from one to another as you knit them on the bias, creating a riot of colors and textures for a dramatic frame. Pockets finish it off. The bias knitting allows the band to be manipulated; it is spread slightly around the outside curve and gathered a bit at the back neck. The crochet edging keeps it all in place, and anchors the band to the coat. If you are not an experienced crocheter and finisher, this might be a good piece to turn over to a professional finisher (check your local knitting store).

BARRY'S VERSION (ABOVE): The base yarn in Laura's coat was indeed as light as air, yet thick. In order to achieve the same gauge, I used Zucca, a spun nylon that is also thick yet light, and mixed it with a matching eyelash in Metal. The Metal worked as a support fiber that allowed me to go up in needle size and still match the gauge. With a solid-colored body, I wanted a splash of color to flow around the face, so I used Dune, with its subtle layering of colors and metallic, as the band. I omitted the pockets and found when I attached the band that it acted more like a collar, with a soft roll at the neck, so I didn't need to topstitch the edge of the band to the body.

Laura's Version

SIZES
Small (Medium, Large, X-Large)

KNITTED MEASUREMENTS
(approx.)
Bust: 40 (44, 48, 52)"
Bottom edge: 48 (52, 56, 60)"

MATERIALS
Prism Yarns
For body:
(A) 6 (7, 8, 9) skeins Mohair (2oz/120yds),
    color Granite
(B) 7 (8, 9, 10) skeins Air (1oz/110yds), color Out of
    Africa
1 pair each of size 13 US and size 15 US needles, or
    size to obtain correct gauge

For bands and pocket:
1 (1, 1, 1½) skein(s) Light Stuff (6-8oz/400yds),
    color Senegal
1 skein Quicksilver (2oz/160yds), color Senegal
1 pair of size 6 US needles or size to obtain correct
    gauge
Size D crochet hook
2 safety pins

GAUGES
11 sts and 14 rows = 4" in stock st and 1 strand A and
    B on size 15 needles
20 sts and 28 rows = 4" in stock st and Light Stuff on
    size 6 needles

NOTE: *Because Air is a chained tube, the end of the yarn
must be knotted every time it is cut to avoid raveling.*

BACK
With size 13 needles and 1 strand each A and B, CO
68 (74, 80, 84) sts. Work 10 rows garter st. Change to
size 15 needles and stock st, dec 1 st at each edge
every 3 (3½, 3½, 4)" 6 times until 56 (62, 68, 72) sts
remain. Cont to 22 (23, 24, 25)" from CO or desired
length to underarm. BO 7 (8, 9, 10) sts at beg of next
2 rows. Cont to 31 (32½, 34, 35)" from CO. BO all sts
firmly.

FRONTS
With size 13 needles and 1 strand each A and B, CO
35 (38, 42, 44) sts. Work 10 rows garter st. Change to
size 15 needles and stock st, dec 1 st at side edge only
every 3 (3½, 3½, 4)" 6 times until 29 (32, 36, 38) sts
remain. When work is 22 (23, 24, 25)" from CO or
desired length to underarm, shape armholes as for
back at side edge, and at the same time, shape neck:
dec 1 st at front edge every third row 8 (9, 10, 10)
times. When piece is same length as back, BO all sts
firmly. Rep for other front, reversing shaping.

SLEEVES

With size 13 needles and 1 strand each A and B, CO 22 (24, 26, 26) sts. Work 10 rows garter st. Change to size 15 needles and stock st, inc 4 sts evenly spaced across next row. Beg inc 1 st at each edge every third row 10 (11, 11, 12) times until there are 46 (50, 52, 54) sts. When sleeve is 17 (18, 18½, 19)" from CO or desired length, shape cap: BO 4 sts at beg of next 8 rows. BO rem sts.

FINISHING

Sew shoulder seams firmly. Sew sleeves into armhole edge between bound-off sts. Sew side and sleeve seam, tacking edge of sleeve to armhole bound-off sts.

TIP
Sew seams with a double strand of Mohair.

BACK NECK SHAPING

With 1 strand each of A and B held together, size 15 needles, and RS facing, pick up and K 18 sts along back neck between shoulder seams. Work short row shaping as follows:

Knit 1 row; turn.

Knit to within 1 st of end; turn.

Knit to within 1 st of end; turn.

Knit to within 2 sts of end; turn.

Knit to within 2 sts of end; turn and cont in garter, working 1 less st to each end for a total of 8 rows; turn.

Knit across all sts, pick up 1 more st in shoulder seam; turn.

Knit across all sts, pick up 1 st in shoulder seam; turn.

Knit across, pick up 1 more st in front; turn.

Knit across, pick up 1 st in front; turn and BO all sts.

Front Band

With size 6 needles and Light Stuff, CO 1 st. Beg bias shaping: inc 1 st at beg and end of first st until there are 3 sts. Work in stock st, inc 1 st at beg and end of next row (WS). Knit 1 row even. Inc at beg and end of next 2 rows until there are 7 sts. Work 1 row even. Cont inc for 2 rows, then work 1 row even until band measures 4 (4¼, 4¼, 5)" along one edge. Beg length: inc 1 st in first st every knit row, and K2tog at end of every knit row. Work entire length of band this way, to approx 76 (80, 84, 86)" along longer edge. Pin band to jacket, on top of body and matching one long edge to front edge. Place a safety pin on band at each shoulder seam. Stretch outside edge of band around back neck so that it lies flat (you will take inside edge in a bit when band is attached). Remove band and cont knitting as necessary to make the long edges even below shoulder-seam pins. When both sides are same length, beg dec 1 st at each edge for 2 rows; work 1 row even (as you shaped the increased end). When 1 st remains, fasten off.

Pockets

Work as for front band until pocket measures 8 (8¼, 8½, 8½)" across. Beg dec immediately (pocket will be square).

Finishing

With Quicksilver and size D crochet hook, work 1 row sc along outside edge of band, placing 1 st in every other row only to keep band flat along front parts, and working a st in every row around neck area (this will help force outside edge to curve).

Tip

The first row of sc sts should actually pull the edge in a bit; the later row of rev sc will spread the edge out. If you are in doubt, work a few inches, then work rev sc along those inches to judge the correct spacing.

Lay band on top of jacket body, lining up the unfinished band edge to front and neck edges of body. Baste with a contrasting thread. Try jacket on to make sure that band lies flat and is not pulling body up. Work a row of sc along bottom and front edges of band, again working a st in every other row of band and working through body as well. Work a row of rev sc back along this edge, then cont along bottom and outside edge of band, keeping band separate from body. Fasten off, leaving a very long tail. With this tail, topstitch band to body, through the "ditch" between crochet rows.

Pockets

With Quicksilver, work 1 round of sc and 1 round of rev sc around entire edge, then leaving a very long tail, fasten off. Pin pocket to body, placing it 2 (2½, 3, 4)" above hem and ½" from front band. Topstitch pocket in place, through the "ditch." Reinforce at corners by stitching 2 or 3 times.

Note: *The pocket may extend over your side seam.*

Barry's Version

MATERIALS

Trendsetter Yarns

Body

(A) 10 (12, 14, 16) balls Zucca (50g/72yds),
 color 5008

(B) 8 (9, 10, 11) balls Metal (20g/90yds), color 248

1 pair each of size 10½ US and size 11 US needles,
 or size to obtain correct gauge

Band

4 (4, 4, 4) balls Dune (50g/90yds), color 80

1 (1, 1, 1) ball Sunshine (50g/95yds), color 8

NOTE: *If pockets are desired, you will need 1 more ball
of Dune and 1 more ball of Sunshine*

1 pair of size 8 US needles

Size E crochet hook

GAUGE

11 sts and 14 rows = 4" in stock st, with 1 strand A
 and B held together on size 10½ needles

DIRECTIONS

Work as for Laura's Version, using yarn substitutions above. For band, work garter st instead of stock st. Pockets are optional.

FINISHING

Assemble as for Laura's Version. For band, attach front edge to body, but do not topstitch long outside edge to body.

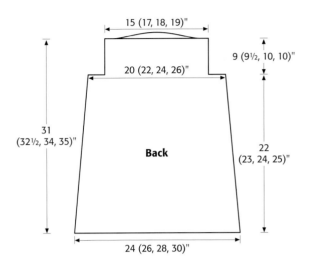

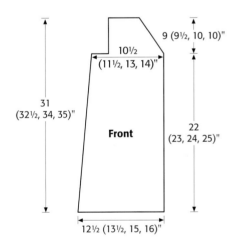

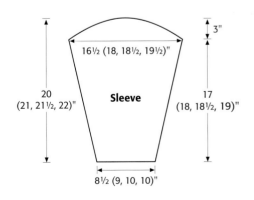

Shine On

Designed by Laura Bryant

MATERIALS

Prism Yarns in a variety of colors, including Tahoe, Harvest, Meadow, and Sierra

1 skein Super Dazzle (1oz/90yds)

1 skein Bon Bon (2oz/94yds)

1 skein ¼" Sparkle Ribbon (2.5oz/90yds)

1 skein Cleo (1.5oz/82yds)

1 skein Sunshine (1oz/65yds)

2 skeins Rococo (3oz/72yds)

1 pair each of sizes 15 US and size 17 US needles

Size K crochet hook

DIRECTIONS

With size 17 needles and ¼" Sparkle Ribbon, CO 130 sts. Change to size 15 needles and another yarn, and cut a 10" tail, tying the next yarn to this one with a 10" tail (making fringe as you go). Work in garter st, dec 1 st at beg of every other row, and inc 1 st at end of same row. Work next row even.

TIP

Mark the dec end with a pin, and when you beg a row on the pin side, you know it is a shaping row.

Change yarns every row, using more of those you have more of. When piece is approx 18" wide, lain flat, and most of the yarns have been used, BO with size 17 needles. With size K crochet hook and Rococo, fasten to beg of long edge and work *ch 3, skip 1 st , sc in next st*; rep from * to * along long edges only. Fasten off, leaving long ends as fringe. Cut rem yarns into 20" lengths for fringe. Tie to short edges in pairs, spread along edge to fill in.

I love wearing dramatic rectangular wraps that showcase beautiful yarns. They are a great accent to any outfit and provide a nice bit of warmth in too-cold air conditioning. These wraps knit up quickly on big needles, and the more textures you choose to put in, the better. Finished with luxurious fringe and sometimes angular shaping at the ends, any one of them would take you through the day and night in style!

Misty Morning Moment

Designed by Laura Bryant

MATERIALS

Prism Yarns

(A) 1 skein ½" Sparkle Ribbon (3.5oz/95yds), color Fog

(B) 1 skein Super Dazzle (1oz/90yds), color Fog

(C) 1 skein Cleo (1.5oz/82yds), color Fog

(D) 2 skeins Charmeuse (1.75oz/68yds), color French Vanilla

(E) 3 skeins Kid Slique (2oz/88yds), color French Vanilla

1 pair each of size 19 US and size 13 US needles

Cable needle

Size N crochet hook

DIRECTIONS

To avoid casting on too tightly, hold a size 13 needle and a size 19 needle together; CO 90 sts with A. Drop the size 13 needle, and change to D and E, cutting A and leaving a tail approx 8" long; leave an 8"-long tail when tying on next yarns (this makes fringe as you go). Work the following rows in garter st:

Row 1: D and E held together

Row 2: E and C held together

NOTE: *Don't cut and add Kid Slique every time, but add other yarns as described above. Kid Slique will fray at ends and does not make good fringe, so when there is a Kid Slique end, tie a tight knot very near cut ends, tying both strands together.*

Row 3: D and E held together

Row 4: E and B held together

Rep these 4 rows 2 more times, then end with 1 more row of D and E.

Next row: With A, knit across, wrapping yarn around needle twice for each st.

CABLE CROSSING

Change to D and E, and K1, dropping extra loop off of needle, *Slip next 2 sts to cable needle and hold in front of work, dropping extra loops off; K2, dropping extra loops off; K2 from cable needle*; rep from * to *, end K1.

Rep entire sequence once more, then rep 13 rows of stripe sequence again. BO with A, holding size 13 needle alongside the 19.

With size N crochet hook and A, work 1 row rev sc along long edges only. Cut rem ribbon into 16" lengths for fringe and add to short edges.

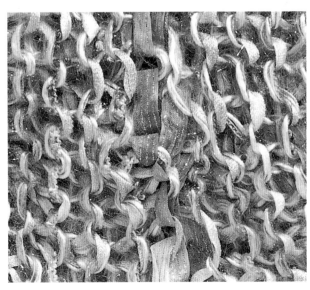

DIRECTIONS

With Impressions, cast on as for Misty Morning Moment wrap. Work garter st until all yarn is used, saving enough for binding off. BO as for Misty Morning Moment wrap.

With 1 strand each color Touch Me, work 1 row sc and 1 row rev sc along each long edge only, leaving 8" long tails when joining and fastening off. Cut rem Touch Me into 16" long strands, and using 1 strand of each color together, tie to short edge of wrap. To keep Touch Me from slipping, pull the entire strand through and double over, then tie with an overhand knot (make a loop and pull the strands through).

Garter Stitch Grandeur

Designed by Laura Bryant

MATERIALS

2 skeins Prism Impressions (6-8oz / 150yds),
    color Yosemite
2 balls Muench Touch Me (1.75oz / 61yds),
    color 3601
2 balls Muench Touch Me, color 3610
1 pair each of size 19 US and size 13 US needles
Size J crochet hook

BARRY'S WRAPS

Waves of Pleasure

Designed by Barry Klein

MATERIALS

Trendsetter Yarns in desired colors

    6 balls Dune (50g/90yds)

    2 balls Balboa (50g/150yds)

1 pair of size 11 US needles

Size F crochet hook

WAVE STITCH

Row 1: (RS) K1, *K1, wrapping yarn 2 times, (K1 wrapping yarn 3 times) 2 times, K1, wrapping yarn 2 times, K2*; rep from * to *.

Row 2: Knit back across row, dropping extra wraps.

Row 3: K1, wrapping yarn 3 times, K1, wrapping yarn 2 times, K2, K1, wrapping yarn 2 times, *(K1, wrapping yarn 3 times) 2 times, K1, wrapping yarn 2 times, K2, K1, wrapping yarn 2 times*; rep from * to *, end K1, wrapping yarn 3 times, K1.

Row 4: Knit back across row, dropping extra wraps.

Rows 5 and 6: Knit back across row.

DIRECTIONS

With Dune, CO 47 sts and knit back across row. Beg wave st, keeping 2 sts at each end in garter st. Work rows 1–4 in Dune and rows 5 and 6 in Balboa. Work in wave st until 78" from beg. Change to Dune and knit 1 row. BO. With size F crochet hook and Balboa, work 1 row sc along bottom edges of scarf. Cut extra Dune and Balboa for fringe and attach through border.

There are endless possibilities when creating these fun wraps. In some cases, I made them shorter as light shoulder wraps and other times longer and thicker with fringe. Because the designs are simple, you can substitute different novelty yarns without worrying about gauge. Wraps can be worked until desired length is reached or you run out of yarn.

Textured Treat

Designed by Barry Klein

SIZES

36" (48", 60")

MATERIALS

Trendsetter Yarns in desired colors

  (A) 2 (3, 4) balls Dune (50g/90yds)

  (B) 2 (3, 4) balls Dolcino (50g/100yds)

  (C) 4 (5, 6) balls Sorbet (50g/55yds)

  (D) 2 (3, 4) balls Zucca (50g/72yds)

1 pair of size 13 US needles

DIRECTIONS

With A, CO 94 (124, 144) sts. Work in garter st, changing colors every 2 rows and cutting fringe and knotting at each end as follows: Knit across row. Leave 6" tail and cut yarn. Leave a 6" starting tail, knot to end tail, knit across row, leave a 6" tail, and cut. Join new yarn and rep process. Tie tails into single knots to secure them. Work, changing colors every 2 rows until 14" from CO. BO loosely.

All Tied Up

Designed by Barry Klein

MATERIALS

Trendsetter Yarns in desired colors
    4 balls Biscotto (50g/55yds)
    1 ball each of 6 colors Dolcino (50g/100yds)
1 pair of size 13 US needles
Size H crochet hook

DIRECTIONS

Unwind and cut each ball of Dolcino into 1½-yard lengths. Put all pieces in a bag and mix them up. With size 13 needles and Dolcino (pre-tie about 6 lengths together, alternating the colors at random), CO 180 sts. Cont to tie Dolcino together and work in patt as follows:

Rows 1 and 2: With Dolcino, knit across.
Rows 3 and 4: With Biscotto, knit across.
Rep rows 1–4 for pattern.

On Dolcino rows, work until 4" of tail remains. Add another piece by placing end of one piece over the other and knotting them together. Allow ends to show on both sides of knitting. Work in patt until 13" from CO. BO loosely in Dolcino.

FINISHING

With size H crochet hook and Biscotto, attach yarn to end of scarf. *Chain 8, skip next 2 sts, and join with sl st to next st along edge*; rep from * to * across long edge. Rep for other long edge. With extra Dolcino only, cut pieces for fringe and attach to ends of shawl as desired.

CONSTRUCTION TECHNIQUES

FINISHING IS THE single most important process to impart a professional look. It pays to practice seaming and edging techniques. Good finishing allows you to perfect the fit and gives the finisher the opportunity to fix anything that might have been missed. Like delicious icing that pulls the layers of a cake together, quality finishing transforms flat pieces into wearable fashion. For best results, you might want to consider having your local store's finisher do the work.

Blocking

We recommend gently blocking each piece with steam after knitting. Use T-pins to keep the pieces flat while you steam. The knitting diagram, with any changes made for custom fit, is a good guide for laying out the pieces, wrong side up. Gently steam the entire surface, paying particular attention to any edges that might be rolling. Do not put the weight of the iron on the pieces. Allow the knitting to dry, then remove the pins.

Side Seams

We prefer seaming vertical seams with the mattress stitch, which is worked from the right side and provides an invisible seam. Some knitters prefer to add two stitches to a pattern to provide for a full stitch being lost at the seams. The patterns in this book include edge stitches.

The mattress stitch is worked from the right side of the knitting. Place the pieces to be seamed on a table, right sides up and aligned along the edge to be seamed. Begin at the lower edge, either with the long tail from casting on or with a firmly anchored length of yarn. If the yarn from the pieces is very nubby or otherwise textured, select a strong, plain yarn of similar color for your seaming. Insert the needle under two horizontal bars between the first and second stitches from the edge, then under two stitches from the other edge. Pull the yarn firmly in the direction of the seam, away from you, then repeat, working from one side to the other. The seam becomes invisible as you pull the yarn.

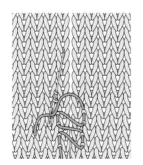

Shoulder Seams

Since novelty yarns often are heavier than traditional plied yarns, special attention needs to be paid to the shoulder, where the weight of the garment will be borne.

Laura binds off the shoulders firmly, then places them right sides together and slipstitches with a crochet hook, under the bound-off edges. She pulls the slip-stitching as tight as necessary to hold the seam with no elasticity. This provides a definite seam line. Once the shoulders are sewn, sew the side seams, the sleeve seams, and then set the sleeve into the armhole.

SLIP-STITCH SHOULDERS

When binding off the shoulders, leave a tail approximately four times the length of the shoulder width. With right sides facing and front on top, insert a crochet hook through both loops of the first bound-off stitch on each piece and pull up a loop of the tail. Insert the hook through both loops of the next two stitches and pull up a loop, then pull this loop through the loop already on the hook. Continue in this manner to the end, working continuously

across the back neck stitches for extra stabilization. Fasten off and weave in the end. You can pull more tightly or loosely as you work, as needed, to stabilize the seam. This is a good way to stabilize an existing sweater whose shoulders have stretched out.

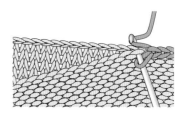

KITCHENER STITCH

Also known as weaving or grafting, the kitchener stitch can be done on a bound-off seam or on loose stitches. We recommend binding off for a shoulder seam, but when there will be no pressure on the join, you can work on live stitches. Then the grafting becomes absolutely invisible, because you are actually inserting a row of knitting with a needle and joining the two existing pieces. You can leave a long tail when you bind off and use this yarn for the seam.

Place the two pieces right sides up on a table, with the edges to be seamed adjacent. With a threaded tapestry needle, insert the needle into the V of the first stitch on the piece nearest you, then into the V of the first stitch of the other piece. Insert the needle through both threads that make the V of the next stitch on the piece nearest you, then through the same V of the other piece. Pull the tension just enough so the stitch you have just made looks like the knitting. Repeat across, then fasten off and weave in the end.

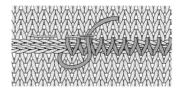

This provides an almost invisible seam, but it may need to be reinforced with a slip stitch on the inside. If you've used very heavy yarns, especially if the garment is a coat or jacket, you may need to hand or machine stitch a piece of twill tape along the shoulder line and across the back neck to stabilize the knitting. Laura's seaming method provides a "ditch" into which machine stitching can be made invisibly. Any shoulder seam should be the desired finished shoulder width, with no stretch allowed.

To sew set-in, inset, or drop-shouldered sleeves to the body, Laura prefers placing right sides together, then slipstitching, evenly (but not tightly), through both layers with a crochet hook, as for the shoulder seam. Laura likes the crispness and definition of the distinct seam line.

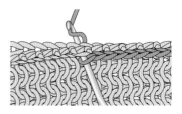

Barry's alternative is to use the mattress stitch along the vertical lines with a variation that combines the mattress stitch along the body piece, then use the kitchener stitch where the cap levels off at the top. This provides a less obvious seam but is not as crisp. Many times novelty yarns have so much interest and texture that an obvious seam isn't very obvious, and the increase in stability can be helpful.

Barry prefers to set the sleeve to the armhole edge before sewing any side seams. After sewing shoulder seams, find the center of the sleeve cap and pin this to the shoulder seam. Beginning at the edge of the sleeve and the beginning of the armhole, with right sides up and edges adjacent, use a mattress stitch where stitches are vertical and a kitchener stitch where stitches are horizontal (such as the top of the sleeve cap). Then sew side and sleeve edges in one continuous seam.

Edgings

One way to customize any garment is to consider the best edging for the yarn you have chosen. Traditional knitting has button and bottom bands of ribbing, but novelty yarns often don't make great ribbings. An alternative to ribbing may make sense, especially if your yarn is textured or lacks elasticity. Many of the patterns in this book use other finishes, and we have chosen the appropriate finish for the yarn specified. If you have substituted yarns, you may need to change your edgings.

RIBBING

Yarns good for ribbing have some elasticity. Traditional plied wool or wool-blend yarns are the best. Cotton yarns, even in a traditional ply, will not have the same effect as wool but can be improved and enhanced by using a twisted rib stitch, where the knit stitches are worked through the back loop. Knitted rayon or nylon tubular tapes, when worked on small needles, work well since the knitted construction adds elasticity. Ribbing usually pulls in and should be used when a bloused look is desired.

Detail of K1P1 rib knit edge

Detail of K2P2 rib knit edge

Garter Stitch, Seed Stitch, and Slip Stitch Variations

These types of stitches flatten the natural curl of stockinette stitch without pulling it in. Novelty yarns lend themselves to this type of edging, as the stitches show off texture well. To change an edging to one of these, you must do a gauge swatch in the desired edge stitch, then compare it to the body gauge. Adjust the number of stitches so that the edge is no larger than the body measurement, preferably about an inch smaller. For example, if the garment body calls for 90 stitches, at 4½ stitches per inch, and the gauge for the seed stitch is the same, reduce the number of stitches for the band by 4 or 5 stitches. These stitches are then increased, evenly spaced, when you begin the body. Sleeve bottoms may need to be even smaller to achieve a cuff effect. Elastic may be added to the inside of sleeve cuffs to pull them in and ensure that they will maintain the required size.

Garter stitch edge

Seed stitch edge

Slip stitch edge
(linen stitch, a type of slip stitch)

CROCHETED EDGINGS

Crochet can be done successfully on pieces that have little natural roll. A simple row of single crochet followed by a row of reverse single crochet, also known as the crab stitch, can be a beautiful finish if the fabric is relatively flat.

Single Crochet

Working from right to left, with the right side of the work facing you, insert a crochet hook into the first knit stitch, draw up a loop, wrap yarn around the hook, and draw it through the loop on the hook (yarn fastened to knitting); *insert the hook into the next stitch, draw up a loop, wrap the yarn around the hook, and draw through both loops (stitch made)*; repeat from * to *. Turn, chain 1, and work more rows as desired, or work one row of reverse single crochet (see next description). When finished, fasten off and weave in the end.

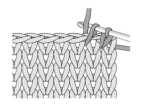
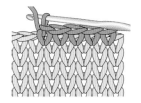

Reverse Single Crochet (Crab Stitch)

This is usually worked on a foundation row of single crochet. Working from left to right, with right side facing, insert the hook into the single crochet stitch to the right, draw up a loop, then wrap and draw through both loops (stitch made). Repeat, moving from left to right. Always keep your hook parallel to the work. If you twist your hand around when inserting the hook, the stitch will not be correct. Notice that keeping your hook parallel to the work is a bit awkward, but it gets easier as you practice. Keeping the tension a bit looser makes it easier to work.

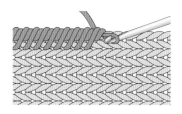

Textured yarns, such as bouclés, and textured stitches that use knits and purls together on the right side, such as seed or linen, will produce relatively flat fabric. If the fabric needs only a little flattening, a couple of extra rows of single crochet may help, but if there is a lot of roll, the edge will still roll where the crochet joins the knitting. Working a row of slip stitch on top of the knitted edge can give a firm foundation on which to build other stitches.

Crocheted stitches are thicker and firmer than knitted stitches, making crocheted edgings a good choice for soft yarns with little body.

Knitted Buttonholes

The type of edging you use will also suggest the type of buttonhole you need. We prefer the single row, self-reinforcing buttonhole as described by Barbara Walker. This is a very stable, firm buttonhole with little tendency to stretch, and thus will not strain the yarn. However, since it does not stretch, this buttonhole needs to be made the correct size for the button. If a buttonhole is too large, a thin elastic can be run around the edge of the hole to help hold the button in place and keep the hole from gaping.

1. Work to buttonhole position, then bring yarn to front of work, slip 1 st from left-hand needle to right-hand needle, pass yarn to back of work, and drop it there. (Do not use yarn for next 2 steps.)

2. Sl another st from left-hand needle to right-hand needle, and pass first st over this st (1 st bound off).

3. Repeat this BO until desired number of sts have been bound off.

4. Slip last bound-off st back to left-hand needle and turn work. Pick up yarn and pass it between the needles to back. CO same number of sts that were bound off for buttonhole, plus 1 more, using cable CO: *insert right-hand needle between first and second sts on left-hand needle, draw through a loop, and sl this loop onto left-hand needle (1 st CO)*; treat this st as the first st, then repeat from * to * until you have CO the same number of sts as you bound off, plus 1.

5. Before placing last st on left-hand needle, bring yarn through to front to form a dividing strand between these 2 sts. Turn work again, then sl first st from left-hand needle to right-hand needle, then pass last (extra) CO st over this st to anchor this end of buttonhole.

Detail of knitted buttonhole

Crocheted Buttonholes

Buttonholes in crocheted edgings are simple and are made by chaining the desired number of stitches and skipping the corresponding stitches in the body. More rows of crochet can be worked after this buttonhole row, working the corresponding number of stitches that were skipped over the loop. This gives a traditional buttonhole look, with the buttonhole in the middle of the band. You may choose to do a button loop on the last row of single crochet, which makes a loop on the very edge. This is attractive when you work a row of reverse single crochet back over the edge and work the number of skipped stitches back over the chain loop.

Detail of buttonhole crochet

Detail of button loop crochet

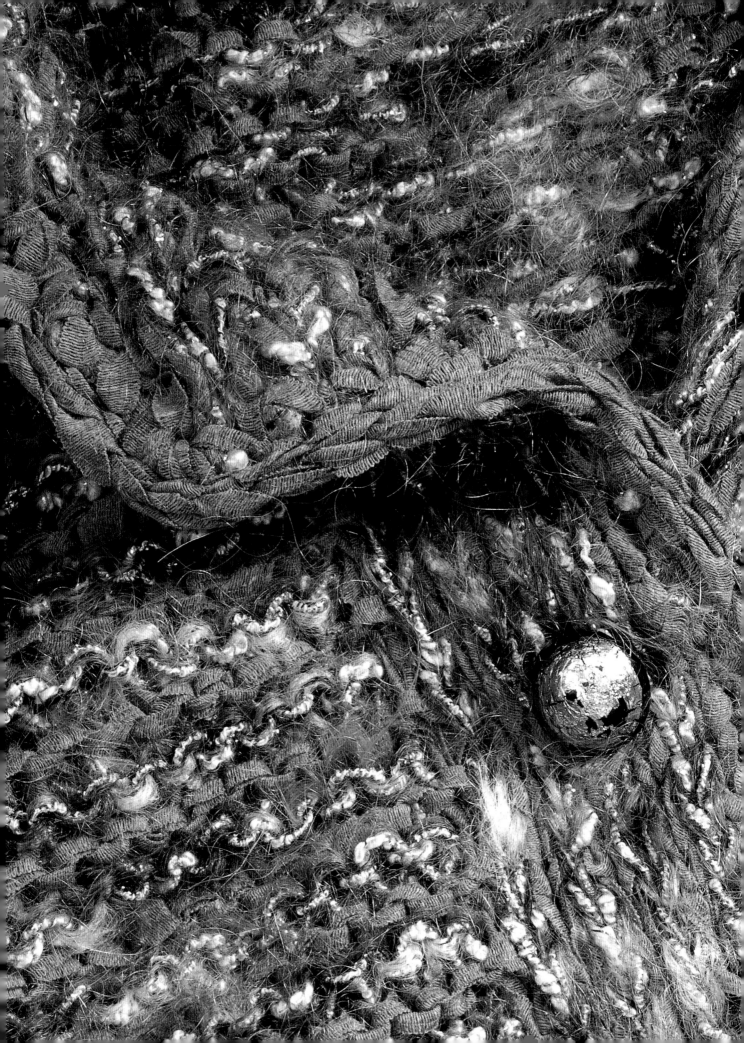

AVOIDING AND FIXING DISASTERS

Careful consideration before seaming and finishing your garment can alleviate disappointment. Once you have blocked your work, remove the pieces and remeasure them. If they are too large, seam in several stitches from the edge, leaving a slightly bulkier seam. Pieces that are too small may be reblocked and gently stretched, although this may make the piece shorter. If the pieces are still not large enough, you can knit a gusset to insert at the side seam. Cast on the desired number of stitches and knit a strip in pattern that can be seamed to both the front and back at the sides. The armhole will become larger, but this can be a good alternative to ripping the entire project.

Once the seams are sewn, but before you make the edgings, try the garment on. Check for drape, where the fronts meet, how the shoulders sit, and where the neck falls. These are easier to alter before edging. If the shoulders are too wide, reinforce them now with either slip stitches or twill tape. Continue either type of reinforcement across the back neck. If the shoulders are too narrow, remove the shoulder seam and reseam it with less tension. If the fronts droop, your bands can compensate by pulling the front edges up. If the garment is too snug or the neck too low, make a wider front or neckband. If the neck is too tight, release some of the shoulder seam at the neck edge and allow some of the shoulder to remain open. Any unevenness can be hidden in the neck finishing. Final finishing should include another session with your steamer. With the garment inside out, gently pat steam onto all seams to flatten them slightly. Pat the neck and front bands, and allow the garment to dry. Voilà! You are successful—your garment is ready to wear!

GLOSSARY AND ABBREVIATIONS

approx—approximately

beg—begin(ning)

BO—bind off

CC—contrast color

CO—cast on

cont—continue

dec—decrease(ing); decrease either by inserting needle into 2 sts at once and knit (or purl) together as one (K2tog or P2tog) or sl 1 as if to knit, K1, PSSO (pass slip stitch over)

Full-fashion dec—*on knit side:* K1, sl 1 as if to knit, K1, PSSO; work across to last 3 sts; K2tog, K1
on purl side: P1, sl 1 as if to knit, P1, PSSO; work across to last 3 sts; P2tog, P1
(This method places the dec inside of the edge stitch. It is sometimes worked with 2 or 3 sts between the edge and the dec.)

garter st—knit every row

inc—increase(ing); increase by working into front and back of same stitch

K—knit

K2tog—knit 2 stitches together through front loops

K2tog-b—knit 2 stitches together through back loops

kitchener st—a method of weaving seams invisibly stitch to stitch; best used on horizontal seams (see page 130)

mattress st—a method of weaving seams invisibly row to row; best used on vertical seams (see page 129)

MC—main color

M1—make 1 stitch (full-fashion increase): make new stitch by lifting up bar between stitches from front to back with left needle and knitting into back of loop

P—purl

patt—pattern

rem—remaining

rep—repeat

rev sc—reverse single crochet

rib—any combination of knits and purls that line up row after row: K1, P1 every row, for example, but may be done in any multiples (K2, P2, etc.)

RS—right side

sc—single crochet

sl st—slip stitch from left to right needle as if to purl unless specified otherwise

space dyed—yarn that has been dyed in multicolors after spinning; colors appear as distinct spaces

st(s)—stitch(es)

stock st—stockinette stitch (knit right-side rows, purl wrong-side rows)

wyib—with yarn in back

wyif—with yarn in front

WS—wrong side

YO—yarn over needle from front to back

RESOURCES

For a list of shops in your area that carry the yarns and buttons mentioned in the book, write to the following companies.

Blue Moon Buttons
406 Mission Street #E
Santa Cruz, CA 95060

Geddes Glass Studio
3259 NE Davis
Portland, OR 97232

Front & Center Buttons
16742 Stagg Street #104
Van Nuys, CA 91406

Prism
2595 30th Avenue North
St. Petersburg, FL 33713

Muench Yarns & Buttons
285 Bel Marin Keys Boulevard
Novato, CA 94949

Trendsetter Yarns
16742 Stagg Street #104
Van Nuys, CA 91406

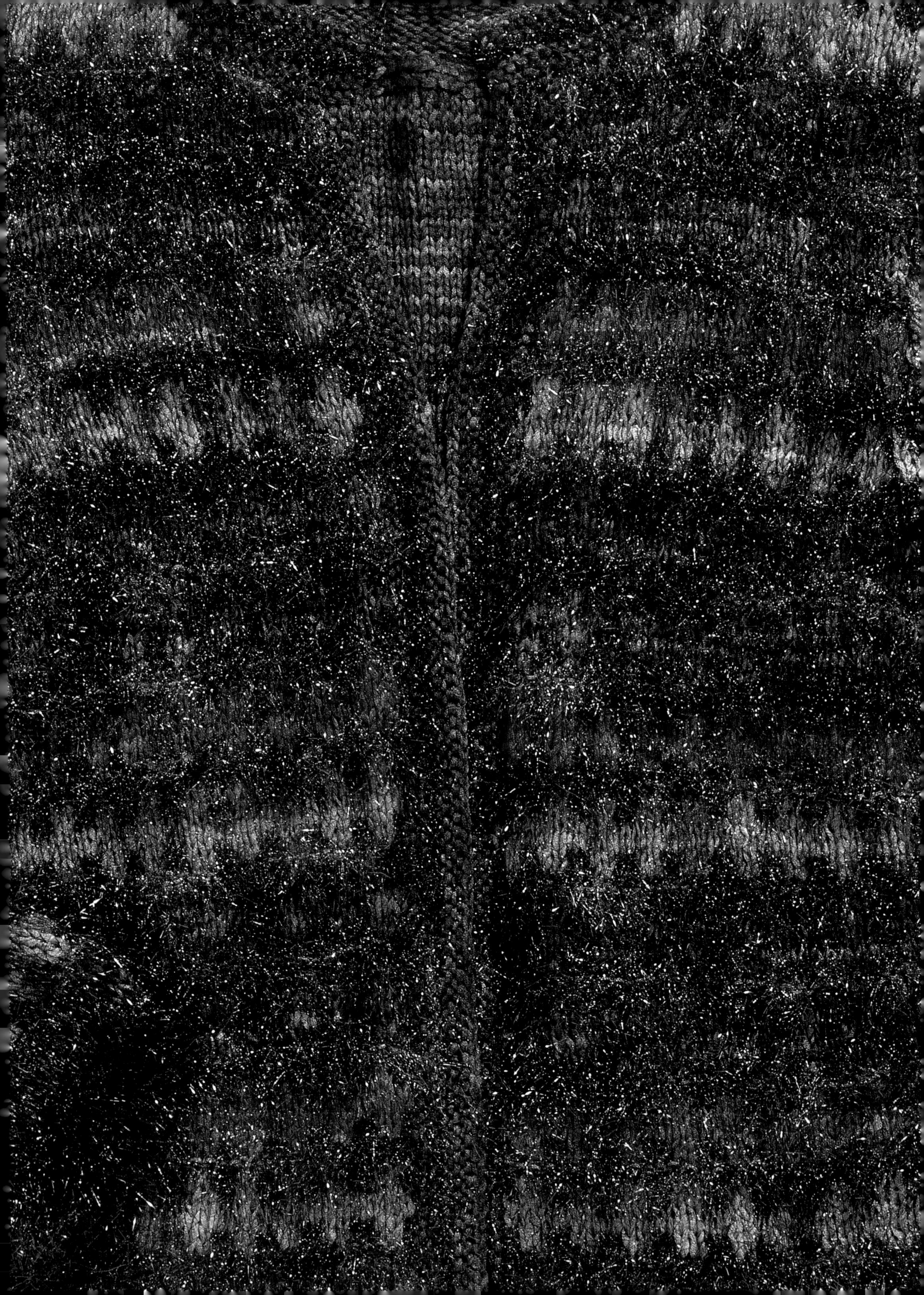

new and bestselling titles from

America's Best-Loved Craft & Hobby Books™

America's Best-Loved Quilt Books®

NEW RELEASES
1000 Great Quilt Blocks
American Stenciled Quilts
Americana Quilts
Appliquilt in the Cabin
Bed and Breakfast Quilts
Best of Black Mountain Quilts, The
Beyond the Blocks
Blissful Bath, The
Celebrations!
Color-Blend Appliqué
Fabulous Quilts from Favorite Patterns
Feathers That Fly
Handcrafted Garden Accents
Handprint Quilts
Knitted Throws and More for the Simply
    Beautiful Home
Knitter's Book of Finishing Techniques, The
Knitter's Template, A
Make Room for Christmas Quilts
More Paintbox Knits
Painted Whimsies
Patriotic Little Quilts
Quick Quilts Using Quick Bias
Quick-Change Quilts
Quilts for Mantels and More
Snuggle Up
Split-Diamond Dazzlers
Stack the Deck!
Strips and Strings
Sweet Dreams
Treasury of Rowan Knits, A
Triangle Tricks
Triangle-Free Quilts

APPLIQUÉ
Artful Album Quilts
Artful Appliqué
Blossoms in Winter
Easy Art of Appliqué, The
Fun with Sunbonnet Sue
Sunbonnet Sue All through the Year

BABY QUILTS
Easy Paper-Pieced Baby Quilts
Even More Quilts for Baby
More Quilts for Baby
Play Quilts
Quilted Nursery, The
Quilts for Baby

HOLIDAY QUILTS
Christmas at That Patchwork Place®
Christmas Cats and Dogs
Creepy Crafty Halloween
Handcrafted Christmas, A
Welcome to the North Pole

LEARNING TO QUILT
Joy of Quilting, The
Nickel Quilts
Quick Watercolor Quilts
Quilts from Aunt Amy
Simple Joys of Quilting, The
Your First Quilt Book (or it should be!)

PAPER PIECING
40 Bright and Bold Paper-Pieced Blocks
50 Fabulous Paper-Pieced Stars
For the Birds
Quilter's Ark, A
Rich Traditions

ROTARY CUTTING
101 Fabulous Rotary-Cut Quilts
365 Quilt Blocks a Year Perpetual Calendar
Around the Block Again
Around the Block with Judy Hopkins
Log Cabin Fever
More Fat Quarter Quilts

TOPICS IN QUILTMAKING
Batik Beauties
Frayed-Edge Fun
Log Cabin Fever
Machine Quilting Made Easy
Quick Watercolor Quilts
Reversible Quilts

CRAFTS
300 Papermaking Recipes
ABCs of Making Teddy Bears, The
Creating with Paint
Handcrafted Frames
Painted Chairs
Stamp in Color
Stamp with Style

KNITTING & CROCHET
365 Knitting Stitches a Year Perpetual
    Calendar
Clever Knits
Crochet for Babies and Toddlers
Crocheted Sweaters
Irresistible Knits
Knitted Shawls, Stoles, and Scarves
Knitted Sweaters for Every Season
Knitting with Novelty Yarns
Paintbox Knits
Simply Beautiful Sweaters
Simply Beautiful Sweaters for Men
Too Cute! Cotton Knits for Toddlers
Ultimate Knitter's Guide, The

Our books are available at bookstores and your favorite craft, fabric, and yarn retailers. If you don't see the title you're looking for, visit us at **www.martingale-pub.com** or contact us at:

1-800-426-3126

International: 1-425-483-3313

Fax: 1-425-486-7596

E-mail: info@martingale-pub.com

For more information and a full list of our titles, visit our Web site.